Ǝ

From
HUE AND CRY
to
HUMBLE PIE

From
HUE AND CRY
to
HUMBLE PIE

Curious, Bizarre and Incomprehensible
Expressions Explained

JUDY PARKINSON

with a Foreword by
ADAM HART-DAVIS

MICHAEL O'MARA BOOKS LIMITED

First published in Great Britain in 2000 by
Michael O'Mara Books Limited
9 Lion Yard, Tremadoc Road
London SW4 7NQ

A CIP catalogue record for this book
is available from the British Library

ISBN 1-85479-581-3

1 3 5 7 9 10 8 6 4 2

Designed and typeset by Martin Bristow

Printed and bound in Finland by WS Bookwell, Juva

FOREWORD

by ADAM HART-DAVIS

Believe it or not, the customer is always right, but don't buy a pig in a poke; look before you leap, or at least take a dekko inside this book. However, I won't beat about the bush; I don't have to sail close to the wind to say it's the bee's knees, the cat's whiskers, the full Monty. It certainly passes the acid test by a long chalk, and the bottom line is that while some of it may be over the top, overall it's finger-lickin' good!

Scientifically, this collection of phrases and sayings is interesting because each one is a 'meme', and a highly successful meme at that. Memes are little bits of information that are passed on from one person to another by imitation; they include phrases, hairstyles, recipes, and tunes. When I sing in my shower, I don't make up my own song, but do my best to imitate one I have heard, perhaps on the radio or from a Beatles album. A song is one kind of meme, and successful songs are the ones we can't get out of our heads.

The world is full of bits of information; think how many words you have read or heard in the last week, on the radio, on television, in newspapers, magazines, and books – thousands of them. All these words and groups of words are memes, and all compete to get into our brains and to get passed on to other people. The fittest memes survive, and the most successful are those that go on being used for years. Clever advertisers are always looking for sparkling new memes, such as 'Liquid engineering' and 'All because the lady loves Milk Tray'. Every phrase in this book, from 'hue and cry' to 'humble pie', is a brilliantly successful meme.

Memes used to be spread only by word of mouth, but then came writing and printing, the telephone, the photocopier and the fax machine, radio and television, and finally the computer and the Internet. Each step has allowed memes to spread faster, further and wider, and some people would go so far as to say that the memes in our brains have driven us to create these pieces of technology – that the Internet is not for our benefit, but for the benefit of the memes, because it allows them to multiply with amazing speed. And yet to create a successful meme still needs a human brain.

I was interested to see in this book that many of the great advertising lines were written by copy-writers who went on to become great authors. Some people seem to have an extraordinary skill in manipulating words so that when they put thousands together they write wonderful books, and when they put a few together in a phrase it acquires exceptional memorability, for that is what makes a great meme. As a result this book is great fun to dip into, and a mine of intriguing information.

So don't fiddle while Rome burns or go off at half-cock; for Pete's sake go for it! Strike while the iron is hot, boldly go, cross the Rubicon, bite the bullet, and put your money where your mouth is. If you buy this book you'll be happy as a sandboy and as pleased as Punch, while if you don't you'll be sick as a parrot and possibly as mad as a hatter. Are you sitting comfortably? Then clear the decks and find out why the curate's egg didn't cut the mustard, why the man on the Clapham omnibus might have a bee in his bonnet, and why the origin of the Elephant and Castle still isn't as plain as a pikestaff.

ADAM HART-DAVIS
June 2000

About one's ears

This colloquialism, which means to be in a very bothersome situation in which one might sustain some pain or trouble, is a shortened form of the proverb, 'To bring a hornets' nest about one's ears'. A hornet is a type of large wasp which can inflict a savage sting; like wasps, but unlike honey bees, hornets can sting repeatedly without damage to themselves. It is well known that bears are very fond of honey, and like Winnie the Pooh have a tendency to make mistakes, and they often get their noses stung by poking their snouts into a hornets' nest mistaking it for a bees' nest. The expression 'To stir up a hornets' nest' implies the same degree of trouble and pain.

According to Cocker

This describes a statement or calculation that is reliably correct. Edward Cocker (1631–75) was a London schoolmaster who published over a hundred editions of his *Arithmetick*, which first appeared in 1678. The phrase was popularized by Arthur Murphy in his farce *The Apprentice* (1756). The American equivalent of the phrase is 'According to Gunter', used to describe a task carefully and correctly done with no chance of a mistake. The English mathematician and astronomer Edmund Gunter (1581–1626) invented 'Gunter's chain', a device used by surveyors to measure distances. A chain is an imperial unit of length equal to 22 yards (66 feet), the actual chain being divided into 100 links each of 7.92 inches; a cricket pitch is 1 chain in length.

According to plan

A well-used expression which is often taken to mean the exact opposite of its apparent meaning. It derives from optimistic communiqués issued during the First World War, often after a particularly bloody or shambolic operation, with the result that the phrase became associated with official attempts to cover up military incompetence and confusion. In true British style, it was thus employed ironically to describe things that did *not* go according to plan. Use of language in this way implies a kind of coded understanding between those in the know, strengthening the sense of camaraderie among those who suffer from such plans.

Acid test, to pass the

Said of someone or something that has been subjected to a conclusive or severe test. Gold is not attacked by most acids, but reacts to nitric acid, also known as *aqua fortis*, which is therefore the acid used in the 'acid test' for gold. To 'put on the acid' is probably derived from 'to pass the acid test' and is Australian slang meaning to exert pressure on someone when asking for a favour or a loan.

Affluent society, the

A phrase, in fashion from the late 1950s, used to describe the growth in material wealth of British society during the decade after the Second World War, with the increasingly widespread ownership of houses, cars, televisions, and items now known as 'white goods' – washing machines, refrigerators, and so on. Health care and other social services were also newly available to all. The term was popularized in JK Galbraith's book *The Affluent Society* in 1958: 'In the affluent society no useful distinction can be made between luxuries and necessities.'

Alive and kicking

Active and in good health. The expression probably refers to a healthy baby either while still in the womb or just after birth. Appropriately, it is the title of a popular Saturday-morning children's show broadcast by BBC Television.

All because the lady loves . . .

A highly successful advertising catch line, originating in the 1960s, for Cadbury's Milk Tray chocolates, which survived all but unchanged for over twenty years and is still quoted today.

Television commercials for Milk Tray featured a mysterious black-clad stunt-man in exotic locations, *au* James Bond, risking life and limb in daring feats to deliver the box of chocolates to his lady love. The clip has been much parodied over the years, perhaps because this series of lavish commercials was used to sell rather ordinary chocolates.

All Greek to me

'It's all Greek to me' is often used to mean that something is completely unintelligible, or is written in a foreign language unknown to the speaker, Greek being particularly tricky to grasp because of its different alphabet. It probably comes from Shakespeare's *Julius Caesar* (1599) in which Casca says, ' For mine own part, it was Greek to me.' Nowadays something incomprehensible is sometimes described as being 'rocket science', while the opposite, 'It's not rocket science,' is often used to indicate that something is simple to grasp. It is also common now to see someone simply passing a hand over his or her head if they find something difficult to understand, a new kind of sign language indicating that something is 'over their head'.

All in a day's work

Said of an unusual or unexpected task that can be obligingly included in the normal daily routine. The expression was common by the eighteenth century, but it is uncertain when it was first coined. A character in Sir Walter Scott's novel *The Monastery* (1820) says, 'That will cost me a farther ride . . . but it is all in the day's work.'

All over bar the shouting

This expression is firmly rooted in the world of sport, and means that victory is in the bag, only the cheering of the crowd at the end of the game or contest being lacking. The phrase may perhaps be derived from boxing, the shouting being the noisy appeal from the supporters of one of the boxers against the referee's decision. It is also often applied to political elections in which the outcome is certain even before the ballot papers have been counted. In a famous reference to the phrase, an excited Kenneth Wolstenholme, the BBC's commentator at the 1966 World Cup final at Wembley, when England won against West Germany, said, 'There are people on the pitch . . . they think it's all over . . . it is now!' In extra time, Geoff Hurst scored a last goal making the final score 4-2 and sealing the Germans' fate. *They Think It's All Over* is now the title of a popular BBC Television sports quiz show.

All singing, all dancing

This piece of popular phraseology was inspired by the first Hollywood musical, *Broadway Melody* in 1929, the era in which sound first came to the movies, which was advertised with posters proclaiming:

The New Wonder of the Screen!

ALL TALKING

ALL SINGING

ALL DANCING

Dramatic Sensation!

The phrase caught on immediately, and two rival studios adopted the same sales pitch in the same year for *Broadway Babes* and *Rio Rita*.

In about 1970 the computing world adopted the phrase to hype up new software, so that by the mid-1980s every kind of organization seemed to boast that their computers and systems packages had some quality that was 'all singing, all dancing'. Also from the mid-1980s the financial world embraced the phrase with enthusiasm to describe the stock market at the time of the 'Big Bang', the major modernization of the London Stock Exchange that came into effect in October 1986. Subsequently the expression has been linked with anything from savings plans, pensions and mortgages to machines – especially electronically controlled machines – of almost any kind. It can just as easily be substituted with the older phrase, 'All bells and whistles', bestowing the 'Wow' factor on almost anything.

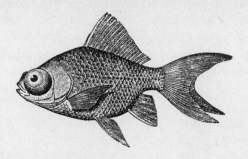

All that glitters is not gold

Appearances are not what they seem. A saying that must have been in use for a thousand years or more and a favourite of poets, it is thought to be Latin in origin. It is a well-known note of prudence in Shakespeare's *The Merchant of Venice* (1596):

> All that glisters is not gold,
> Often have you heard that told.

This implies that the proverb dates from earlier wisdom; certainly it was used by Chaucer in *The Canterbury Tales*, for in 'The Canon's Yeoman's Tale' (*c.* 1387) he wrote:

> However, all that glitters is not gold,
> And that's the truth as we're often told.
>
> (Modern translation by Nevill Coghill, 1951)

Thomas Gray (1716–71) wrote in his 'Ode on the Death of a Favourite Cat, Drowned in a Tub of Gold Fishes'(1747):

> Not all that tempts your wand'ring eyes
> And heedless hearts, is lawful prize;
> Nor all that glisters gold.

While, more cynically, Ogden Nash (1902–72) observed in 'Look What You Did, Christopher':

> All that glitters is sold as gold.

Alternative medicine

The concept of turning away from traditional forms of medicine took hold in the late 1960s. Many people think that there are other ways to treat illnesses and injury other than by long-accepted 'doctor's' methods employing drugs, surgery and so on, and such remedies as homeopathy and acupuncture are widely used today. The word 'alternative' has been applied since the late 1960s to describe some cultural or other value that is different from the norm. Earlier in the decade, in what came to be known as the 'counter-culture' or 'underground', there was much experiment into creating alternative societies, which attempted to exist without most of the accepted appurtenances of modern life. 'Alternative' was applied in the 1980s to a style of comedy which, with its subversive and surreal themes and anti-establishment tone, became widely popular – to the extent that 'traditional' comedy is arguably now 'alternative' itself.

And now for something completely different

An almost ubiquitous British catchphrase of the 1970s that came from *Monty Python's Flying Circus*, a cult comedy television series of the 1960s and 1970s, first broadcast in 1969, which had a huge following of youthful fans who would quote its lines in schools and colleges and at work on the day after each screening of the programme. The phrase was also the title for the *Monty Python* team's first feature film in 1971. In the television show the line was spoken by John Cleese, wearing a dinner jacket and seated at a desk behind a microphone, in a parody of the early BBC announcers, although Cleese's desk would be set in absurd surroundings such as on a beach or hillside. The expression had previously been used on television magazine programmes as a jolly link between two unconnected items, but scriptwriters had to think of something completely different to say after *Monty Python*.

Annus horribilis
A particularly bad or miserable year, the phrase being Latin for 'horrible year'. It owes its popularity to the Queen, who used it in a speech at a banquet in the Guild Hall, London, in 1992, the year which saw the divorce of the Princess Royal, the separations of the Prince and Princess of Wales and of the Duke and Duchess of York, and the devastating fire at Windsor Castle. The next day, the punning headline writers had a **field day** (q.v.), with the *Sun* proclaiming on the front page, 'One's Bum Year'. Conversely, a glorious year can be described as *annus mirabilis*, used to describe 'a year of wonders, catastrophes or other notable events'. One such (for the British, at least) was 1757, which marked Britain's final conquest of Canada and the foundation, again by force of arms, of her Indian empire. Philip Larkin wrote a poem entitled 'Annus Mirabilis' about the year 1963 – see **The birds and the bees** (q.v.).

Ants in one's pants
Said of an excessively restless or eager person, someone displaying such behaviour can also be described as a 'fidget-bottom'. The expression was popularized by Hugh S Johnson, the dynamic former US Army general who was in charge of the National Recovery Administration in 1933–4, when the national reconstruction policies of President Franklin D. Roosevelt's 'New Deal' were implemented. ('Pants' in this case has the American meaning of trousers.) In Britain nowadays the word 'pants' is often used colloquially to mean naff or not very good, possibly harking back to the grubby English sense of the word 'pants'.

An apple a day keeps the doctor away
A popular panacea that holds that to include an apple in the daily diet will guarantee good health. The proverb is said to be of nineteenth-century origin and has no particular medical support, although apples do contain vitamins and fibre, which are part of the daily dietary requirements. However, the American statesman, writer, philosopher and scientist, Benjamin Franklin (1706–90) is credited with quoting the phrase, if not with inventing it, in the eighteenth century.

Apple of one's eye
The Bible has:

> He kept him as the apple of his eye
>
> Deuteronomy 32: 10

and:

> Keep me as the apple of the eye, hide me under the shadow of thy wings
>
> Psalms 17: 8

and:

> For he that toucheth you toucheth the apple of his eye
>
> Zechariah 2: 8

while in Shakespeare's *A Midsummer Night's Dream* (*c.* 1594) we find:

> Flower of this purple dye,
> Hit with Cupid's archery,
> Sink in apple of his eye.

The earliest recorded examples of the phrase's use in this country can be found in the works of King Alfred, dating from the end of the ninth century. At this time, the pupil of the eye was thought to be a solid object, and was known as the 'apple', presumably because an apple was a common spherical object. (Interestingly, the fruit of the Tree of the Knowledge of Good and Evil, which brought about the downfall of Adam and Eve, and which gave rise to our expression 'forbidden fruit' meaning any illicit indulgence or pleasure, has for centuries been represented as an apple. In fact, the Book of Genesis, where the tale is found, does not describe the fruit at all.)

Our modern word 'pupil' comes from Latin and appeared in English in the sixteenth century. It is figurative in origin; the late Latin original was *pupilla*, little doll, which is a diminutive form of pupus, boy, or *pupa*, girl (the source for the other sense of 'pupil', meaning a schoolchild, is the classical Latin *pupillus*, *pupilla*, meaning an orphan or ward, and hence a student taught by a teacher). The word might have been applied to the dark central portion of the eye within the iris because of the tiny image of oneself, like a puppet or marionette, that can be seen when looking into another person's eye.

'The apple of one's eye' is what one cherishes most. As has been said, the pupil of the eye has long been referred to as the 'apple' because it is perfectly round and appears solid. Because sight is so precious, someone who was called this as an endearment was similarly precious, with the result that the phrase took on the figurative sense we still retain.

Apple-pie order
Said of something that is perfectly ordered or set out, or in perfect condition. It is uncertain how this phrase entered the language, although there are various theories. It may have originated as a corruption of the French *cap à pie*, meaning 'head to foot', used to describe a correctly dressed or armed gentleman or soldier. Another suggested French source is *nappes pliées*, 'folded linen', which could therefore be extended to mean 'in perfect order', but it is more likely that it refers to the prank of making an 'apple-pie bed'. Equally, however, the phrase may come from America, where apple pie, the family favourite 'just like Mom used to bake', symbolizes all that is wholesome and homely.

Are you sitting comfortably?
The cosiest question known to the generation that grew up in the 1950s, when radio was still much more common than television. 'Are you sitting comfortably? Then I'll begin . . .' was the line that introduced the regular story in the BBC children's radio programme *Listen with Mother*, and it continued in use until 1982.

Julia Lang, the original presenter, first broadcast the programme in 1950, although there is some dispute as to whether the question was formulated by Lang herself or by Frieda Fordham, an analytical psychologist and adviser to the BBC.

As every schoolboy knows
This is a rather condescending put-down, said as a rejoinder to someone who has said something that is already considered common knowledge. The expression is particularly associated with Lord Macaulay (1800–59), although it had been recorded much earlier. In 1840 one of Macaulay's contemporaries, Lord Clive, wrote:

> Every schoolboy knows who imprisoned Montezuma, and who strangled Atahualpa.

It is, however, doubtful whether many schoolboys today would actually know these facts. In *The Anatomy of Melancholy* (1621) Robert Burton (1577–1640) wrote, 'Every schoolboy hath . . .', while Bishop Jeremy Taylor (1613–67) used the expression 'Every schoolboy knows it' in 1654. Later Jonathan Swift (1667–1745) wrote in his 'The Journal' (1727):

> How haughtily he lifts his nose,
> To tell what every schoolboy knows.

Curiously, 'school' derives from the Greek word *skhole*, meaning 'leisure spent in the pursuit of knowledge', since only those who enjoyed a life of leisure had the time to attend a school. The archetypal prep-school boy, Nigel Molesworth, the inspired creation of Geoffrey Willans and Ronald Searle who first appeared in *Down With Skool!* in 1953, tends to use the expression 'As any fule kno . . .'

Ass in a lion's skin, an

An old saying to describe a cowardly person who blusters or tries to bully others; otherwise, a fool with groundless aspirations to wisdom. The ass in this context represents a fool, an ass or donkey being often used figuratively to symbolize ignorance or stupidity. (In American usage, however, 'ass' equates with English 'arse' – see next.) The legendary allusion is to the fable of the ass that dressed in a lion's skin, but betrayed itself by its braying.

Ass, to cover one's

A slang term, American in origin, meaning to make up an excuse or prepare an alibi in advance, in order to avoid being blamed if something goes wrong. The phrase originated in the 1960s among US troops in Vietnam, and later became part of colloquial American language. It came to Britain in the 1980s, and was probably popularized by its use in the vulgar banter of 'get-rich-quick' financial traders. It is commonly used today in the planning of business ventures or in contracts, in which 'ass-covering clauses' are often included as a means of safeguarding the signatory against the unexpected, and thus blame. The phrase originally derives from military tactics, when one soldier provides covering fire for another as the latter advances; US black slang often uses 'ass' for the self, as in 'I'm going to whup your sorry ass.'

At this moment in time

This roundabout expression, beloved of journalists, commentators and pundits of all shades since the 1960s, is a classic example of a speaker or writer going round the houses and using a circumlocution to make a point with as many words as possible when one word would do – and that word is 'now'.

Aunt – My giddy aunt

An exclamation of surprise, a mild oath. There seems to have been a fashion at the end of the nineteenth century for using the word 'giddy' in a hyperbolical sense. In Kipling's *Stalky & Co* (1899) we find:

> King'll have to prove his charges up to the giddy hilt.

However, it has also been suggested that the expression derives from the archetypal saga of giddy-auntdom, the classic farce *Charley's Aunt* by Brandon Thomas (1856–1914), first performed in 1892:

> I'm Charley's aunt from Brazil – where the nuts come from.

This use of 'giddy' in the phrase ('Oh my sainted aunt' is another variant) suggests something or someone lightheartedly or exuberantly silly, a sense of the word that dates from the sixteenth century, as in the expression 'to act the giddy goat'. Although 'giddy' has been used for hundreds of years in this sense, at first it literally meant to be possessed by a god, and only later shifted to its modern sense of experiencing vertigo or dizziness.

Aunt Sally

An 'Aunt Sally' is a name for anyone or anything that is an object of ridicule or abuse, or of an unreasonable attack. This somewhat cruel term comes from a game, often found at fairgrounds and village fêtes, in which short sticks are thrown at a wooden figure of an old-woman's head mounted on a pole, the fun being to knock off its nose or break the pipe stuck in its mouth. The word 'aunt' was traditionally applied to any old woman; hence in Shakespeare's *A Midsummer Night's Dream* (c. 1594) Puck speaks of, 'The wisest aunt telling the saddest tale'. As an aside, an 'Aunt Emma' is someone who is an unadventurous croquet player.

Awkward age, the

The age of adolescence, when one is no longer a child but not quite an adult, a time when the hormones are said to be jumping. (A modern lighthearted description of teenagers suggests that they are 'hormonally challenged', a parody of many terms derived from 'political correctness'.) Henry James wrote a novel of this title, published in 1899, about a young Englishwoman's emergence from this age into maturity and understanding (though what was particularly awkward for her was that she and her mother were rivals in love for the same young man). The word awkward is applied to other situations involving the young. The 'awkward squad' is the term used to describe young untrained military recruits not yet ready to take their place in the ranks.

Back burner, to put on a (or the)
To put off or postpone. A very useful expression in business if a decision cannot be made immediately, meaning that an idea, proposition, course of action or project can be put aside and kept in reserve for use when necessary, or when circumstances are more propitious. (An almost diametrically opposed metaphor is also used, for an idea or project can be also 'put on ice', to be figuratively defrosted at a later date.) The back burners, or rings, on a cooker are used for simmering, while the front burners are usually the hottest and are used for fast cooking. There is now even a verb form gaining increasing usage, with people talking of 'back-burnering' something.

Back of beyond, the
This is an Australian expression, nineteenth-century in origin, which is now commonly used to describe any remote area, but which originally referred to the vast spaces of the interior of the country, the Great Outback. The 'back', reduced from 'back

country', is the outlying territory behind the settled regions, and the term 'backblock' is found in 1850, referring to those territories of Australia split up by the government into blocks for settlement. The more isolated and sparsely populated areas of the Australian interior are also known as 'the bush'.

Back to basics

This infamous phrase, meaning to go back to the ground rules, to 'traditional values', was first heard in politics in the 1950s. It probably derived from the expression, used in mathematics and physics, 'to go back to first principles', with its implication that any calculation, however complicated, has its origin in just a few essential basic rules. 'Back to basics' was taken up by the Conservative Party in 1993 as an all-embracing political slogan designed to promote family values. John Major, the Prime Minister, launched this ill-fated phrase, albeit with the best of intentions, in a speech to the Conservative Party Conference in 1993:

> The message from this conference is clear and simple. We must go back to basics. The Conservative Party will lead the country back to these basics, right across the board: sound money, free trade, traditional teaching, respect for family and the law.

The campaign soon backfired, not least because of a number of widely publicized sex scandals, characterized as 'sleaze' by the press, within Mr Major's party. In America the phrase 'Back to the basics' was used in the mid-1970s as a government-education slogan to promote better teaching of reading, writing and arithmetic.

Back to square one

To begin again, or, less formally, 'Back to where you started, sunshine!' This colloquialism possibly derives from board games in which players, through bad luck or bad judgement, have to move their pieces back to the starting point. Another suggestion is that it comes from the early days of radio football commentaries, for which diagrams of the pitch divided into numbered squares were printed in radio listings magazines so that listeners could follow the game. The meaning is similar to 'Back to the drawing board', which means to go back and rethink a complete project or scheme. Aircraft designers during the Second World War used the latter phrase when a concept or even a whole design for a new machine proved unworkable and had to be started all over again.

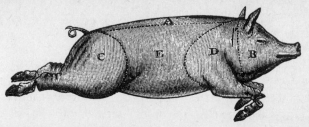

Bacon, to save one's
To have a narrow escape, to emerge from some dire situation without injury or loss. This expression may date from the late seventeenth or early eighteenth century, long before refrigeration, when the meat of the pig was cured and preserved for use during the winter months, and may refer to the need for cured bacon to be protected from any thieving dogs. In his unfinished epic *Don Juan* (1819–24), Lord Byron makes reference to this:

> But here I say the Turks were much mistaken,
> Who hating dogs, yet wish'd to save their bacon.

Bacon was a significant ingredient in the diet of the eighteenth century and the expression 'To bring home the bacon', meaning to earn the money to maintain the household, describes the custom at country fairs of greasing a live pig and letting it loose among a group of blindfolded contestants. He who successfully caught the greased pig could keep it and so 'bring home the bacon'. According to Nathan Bailey's *Universal Etymological English Dictionary* of 1720, 'bacon' was a slang term to describe booty of any kind which fell to beggars, shoplifters, highwaymen and the like in their enterprises; 'to save one's bacon', therefore, was to save something that was valuable both literally and figuratively.

Ballpark figure
Another North Americanism that has taken hold in Britain, this is an estimate, or a budget figure, which might better be described as a 'guesstimate'. A ballpark is a large stadium in America or

Canada built specifically for the game of baseball. The original reference in financial quotations to two or more figures as being 'in the same ballpark' means that they are of roughly the same amount; even so, given that actual ballparks are vast, the variation between such figures may be correspondingly large. 'Ballpark' is also used to describe a situation or state of affairs, as in 'This is a whole new ballpark for me.'

Ban the bomb

This simple, alliterative and easily remembered political slogan first became current in the early 1950s in America. It was taken up in Britain by 1958, when it was used to promote the Campaign for Nuclear Disarmament (CND) during the years of the perceived global threat from nuclear weapons following the increased nuclear tension during the period, known as the Cold War, which succeeded the end of the Second World War. It entered public consciousness by its simplicity, the political correctness of its message, and the striking symbol that went with it, which was seen on almost every surface during the 1960s from T-shirts to brick walls. Both the phrase and the symbol are still in active use today, linked with support for campaigns for nuclear disarmament all over the world.

Bandwagon, to climb on the

To declare support for a popular movement or trend with the intention of profiting or reaping some sort of easy material gain, usually without believing in the movement or trend. The expression is believed to have originated in the Southern States of America, probably dating from the first presidential campaign of William Jennings Bryan (1860–1925) in 1892, when candidates for political elections would parade through the streets led by a band of musicians performing on a large horse-drawn dray. As a publicity stunt the local candidate would mount the wagon as it passed and ride through his constituency with the band as they played, in an attempt to gain personal support from the voters. Bryan never won the presidency, losing to McKinley in 1896 and

1900, and to Taft in 1908; he was, however, appointed Secretary of State in 1913, but resigned from the government in 1915, believing that President Wilson's policies would bring the United States into the First World War, a bandwagon he did not wish to climb on.

Bank – To laugh all the way to the bank

The original expression was 'To cry all the way to the bank', which was a popular catchphrase in the 1950s. It is an ironic comment, usually made about someone who has done something questionable, or produced something kitsch or tasteless or for some other reason generally disapproved of, while making a great deal of money from it. It may have been first said by the high-camp pianist and entertainer Liberace (born Wladziu Valentine Liberace, 1919–87), after a critic had savaged his playing – which was extravagantly ornamented with trills and arpeggios – and his embellished stage act. Liberace was the highest-paid entertainer in the United States during the 1960s and 1970s, and his income averaged $5 million a year for more than twenty-five years. 'To laugh all the way to the bank' was, for him, an obvious twist to the original phrase, as well as a derisive riposte to the critic.

Bark up the wrong tree, to

To be totally off the mark, to waste energy following the wrong course of action, or to have one's attention diverted off the subject in hand. The phrase comes from the American sport of racoon hunting, which generally takes place at night. The hounds of the hunting pack are trained to mark the tree in which the racoon they are pursuing takes shelter, and then to howl at its base until their master arrives to shoot the animal. The hounds will frantically bark up at the wrong tree, however, if they mistake it in the dark. The expression neatly puns a dog's bark and tree bark, and first became popular in the early nineteenth century, appearing in the works of James Hall, Davy Crockett – a great racoon hunter – and Albert Pike.

Bath – To take an early bath

This euphemism comes from the sports pitch, and means to retire early to the dressing room after being injured, or sent off by the referee, during a match of football or rugby. The phrase was popularized from the 1970s by the television sports commentator Eddie Waring in his descriptions of Rugby  League matches, and is now often used to describe any situation in which someone is obliged to pull out of the action before it is over. In America, and increasingly in this country, 'To take a bath' means to suffer any kind of defeat or serious loss, as in 'He took a bath in the stock-market collapse.'

Be like Dad, keep Mum

The British weakness for puns ensured that this expression gained wide currency during the Second World War. 'To keep mum' means to keep a secret or simply to keep quiet, not giving away what you know. In its original context the word 'mum' represented an inarticulate sound made with sealed lips, and 'mumble' probably has the same derivation. In *Henry VI*, Part II Shakespeare has:

> Seal up your lips and give no word but mum.

By the same token, mumchance is a game of dice during which complete silence is maintained. In its other meaning, 'Mum' is a diminutive of 'Mummy', a child's affectionate word for 'mother'.

The slogan itself originated in 1941 on a poster issued by the British Ministry of Information, the body largely responsible for issuing wartime propaganda. The aim was to make sure that people remembered national security and did not engage in idle gossip, which might be overheard by spies. Similar slogans of the war years were 'Careless talk costs lives' and **'The walls have ears'** (q.v.). Unlike the other slogans, however, the five words paint a picture of a bygone age and the sort of life Dad might have expected to lead with Mum, provided she stayed at the kitchen sink.

Beam ends, to be on one's

To be destitute, or nearly so. This is one of many English phrases that describe an extremely impecunious state; others include 'boracic', from Cockney rhyming slang 'boracic lint', meaning 'skint'; to be 'in Carey Street', that street being the site of the old Bankruptcy Courts in the City of London; and to be 'on one's uppers', the upper being the part of the shoe above the sole which covers the upper part of the foot, the phrase implying extreme destitution because one cannot afford to replace the worn-out sole, much less the whole pair of shoes. The origin of the phrase 'on one's beam ends' is not altogether certain, but it probably refers to the beams of a wooden ship, which run across the vessel from side to side, supporting the deck. If the beams are 'on end', then the ship has turned over on its side and cannot right itself – a desperate plight (as is being flat broke).

Beam me up, Scotty

A catchphrase, widely used and held in great affection, this comes from the popular television science-fiction series *Star Trek*, first shown in 1966. Whenever one of the intrepid adventurers from the Starship *Enterprise* found himself in a spot of trouble while away from the ship, he would call up Scotty, the *Enterprise's* chief engineer, to transfer him, as 'matter', back to base. The expression is still widely used, always humorously and often ironically, to mean 'I don't want this task' or 'I don't want to be here'. It enjoys wide currency largely because the TV series is repeated regularly, and also because *Star Trek* has a huge following of fans, who are known as 'Trekkies'.

Beans, to spill the
The expression means 'to let on', to tell all, perhaps prematurely, to an eager audience, to give away a secret or to let the cat out of the bag (see **A pig in a poke**, q.v.). There are various explanations for the derivation, one of the most likely being that it may have originated at the turn of the twentieth century as a colourful American euphemism for vomiting, because beans represented basic food.
The phrase thus roughly equates to 'Cough it up' or 'Spit it out', said when someone is having difficulty in finding the right words, and meaning, 'Be clear, let's have it'. This expression, with its overtones of there being a juicy piece of gossip in the offing, obviously alludes to hiding something in the mouth, and being reluctant to reveal it. Beans appear in various expressions: 'to be full of beans' means to be in high spirits or full of energy, and was originally said of lively horses; beans used to be slang for money or property, so that 'I haven't got a bean' means that one is broke.

Beat about the bush, to
To approach a matter indirectly or in a roundabout way. The reference is probably to a form of hunting in the fifteenth-century, known as 'batfowling', in which one hunter held a light to dazzle the birds roosting in thickets while another went in to seize them – normally the noise of men crashing about in undergrowth would scare the birds out long before the hunters could get near them. Other ancient methods were to disturb the roosting birds in the bush and then catch them in a net as they fluttered out. The hunters would literally beat about all the bushes in order to catch just a few birds.

Bed of nails, to lie on
A situation or position, usually self-inflicted, that is fraught with a multitude of painful or difficult problems. The phrase refers to the spiked bed of the Hindu fakir (ascetic or holy man), but while the spikes may not hurt the fakir, they would be unbearable for most normal mortals. The saying is sometimes used in it variant

26

form, 'to lie on a bed of thorns'. It is thought that the expression first received wide notice in a modern context when it was used by the Labour government in 1966.

Bee in one's bonnet, to have a

To be obsessed with a particular idea or notion, as though mentally all a-buzz. The expression, in the variant 'to have bees in the head', implying scattiness, was in circulation in the sixteenth century, for a reference to bees and crazed thought was recorded by the English poet, Court musician and entertainer John Heywood (c. 1497–c. 1580) in 1546 in one of his collections of English proverbs. A slightly worse accusation current then was 'to have maggots in the head', which meant to suffer complete madness. It is thought that bees met bonnets in the poem 'Mad Maid's Song' by Robert Herrick (1591–1674), written in 1648:

> For pity sir, find out that bee,
> Which bore my love away.
> I'll seek him in your bonnet brave,
> I'll seek him in your eyes.

Beer and sandwiches

This is a political snack, originally consumed during informal negotiations with the Labour ministers and Prime Ministers of the 1960s and 1970s. During the then frequent industrial disputes the phrase became associated with last-ditch talks held between trade-unionists and politicians at No. 10 Downing Street in an effort to avert a threatened strike. This proletarian-style 'pub grub' was looked upon as indicating the high seriousness and impeccable Socialist credentials of the politicians, as well as being thought – rather patronizingly – as being eminently suitable for the 'cloth-cap' negotiators, a sort of working-man's 'champagne and chicken'. A 'beer-and-sandwich' meeting implied (or so it was hoped) that here were honest men in their shirtsleeves, too busy and too honourable to indulge in the lavish and bibulous feasts enjoyed by lesser politicians and union leaders. These days the 'rubber-chicken circuit' describes the usual menu for the rounds of dinners prospective MPs attend in order to woo local party workers and other supporters.

Before you come up
Used in the context, 'I'd stuck my bayonet up twenty-five Jerries before you come up', this was one-upmanship at its worst. With this not altogether hospitable welcome, First World War veterans would attempt to put down greenhorns, young soldiers new to the front line. The phrase implied that the target of the remark was utterly wet behind the ears and would be unlikely to cope with the unpleasant conditions in the trenches. Variations included, 'Before your number [painted on your kitbag] was dry' and 'Before you knew what a button stick [issued to each new recruit] was'.

Believe it or not!
This catchy slogan originated as the title of a cartoon strip created by the American writer Robert Leroy Rinpley (1893–1949) in 1923, with which it is always associated. The concept of the series was to illustrate amazing but allegedly true facts and stories. Later spin-offs from the strip were a radio and television series, and even a museum at Niagara Falls. The phrase is often used ironically, implying that the listener won't believe what is said anyway, whether it is true or not.

Bell – As the bell clinks, so the fool thinks
A foolish person believes what he desires. In the fifteenth-century tale of Dick Whittington, the young poor boy came to London because he believed its streets to be paved with gold and silver. Running away from his cruel master, he reached Highgate Hill where, hungry and tired, he did not know whether to continue his flight from the city. Bow Bells began to ring and the boy imagined that they said, 'Turn again, Whittington, thrice Lord Mayor of London.' The bells clinked their answer to his thoughts and he returned to prosper as a merchant and to become mayor three times. The story is based on a certain Richard Whittington (c. 1358–1423) who came from Gloucestershire to achieve fame and fortune as a merchant and as Lord Mayor

of London – and, not least, ultimately to become a pantomime legend. Dying childless, he left all his money to charity, while the legend of his cat is a long-established part of English folklore.

Best bib and tucker

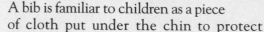

This is probably an old wives' expression, and one that has been addressed to women and children for two or three hundred years. To put on one's best bib and tucker means to don one's 'Sunday best', to make oneself smart and spruce. A bib is familiar to children as a piece of cloth put under the chin to protect clothes while eating, while a tucker was an ornamental frill of lace or linen worn by women in the seventeenth and eighteenth centuries over the bodice to cover the neck and shoulders. This meaning predates the Australian slang word 'tucker' for food, referring to the contents of a tuck box, although there is also a close connection with 'bib and tucker' in this sense.

Best of British luck

Often shortened to 'Best of British', this is an ironic quip as if to say, 'You can get on with it, but leave me out.' It was frequently heard during the early days of the Second World War, when the Allies were losing confidence in their ability to win the war and British luck was hard to come by. It compares with an ironic line from a First World War soldiers' song:

Over the top with the best of luck
Parley voo . . .

(see **Over the top**, q.v.). In the 1960s, 'And the best of British' took on a less sarcastic and more positive meaning, especially with the government-supported 'I'm Backing Britain' campaign. The expression became one of comedian Frankie Howerd's (1917–92) innuendo-laden catchphrases. For instance, when introducing a mock opera he would say,

. . . Vera would pause for breath before a high C and as she mustered herself for this musical Everest I would mutter, 'And the best of British luck!'

Bets – To call off all bets

A summons to cancel all wagers in certain circumstances, deriving from the race track and the betting shop; for instance, a bookmaker may call off all bets if he suspects that a race or other contest has been rigged. In a widening of its meaning, the phrase is used to mean rejecting a complicated or disadvantageous issue. In American black slang of the 1940s, however, it meant to die – indeed, the most final way of calling off all bets.

Big Apple, the

The well-known nickname for New York City. The name was first coined in the 1920s by John J Fitzgerald, a reporter for the *Morning Telegraph*, who used it to refer to the city's race tracks and who claimed to have heard it used by black stable hands in New Orleans in 1921. Black jazz musicians in the 1930s took up the name to refer to the city, especially Harlem, as the jazz capital of the world. The epithet was revived in 1971 as part of a publicity campaign by Charles Gillett, in charge of a push to attract tourists to New York, who was possibly inspired by the name of the Beatles' trading company, the Apple Corporation, founded in 1968. The general allusion is to a city that is the 'big apple' sought as the ultimate location for anyone seeking world fame. There are many classical references to apples, such as the golden apples given by Venus to Melanion so that he could beat, by trickery, the fleet-footed Atalanta in a race; the girl stopped to pick up the apples, and so lost the race and married Melanion. The sentiment behind 'The Big Apple', however, is more likely to be the idea of an apple as a symbol of the best, as in **the apple of one's eye** (q.v.), meaning someone or something that is very precious.

In the eighteenth century, the writer and politician Horace Walpole (1717–97) referred to London as 'The Strawberry', impressed by its freshness and cleanliness compared with foreign cities; he named his estate at Twickenham, Middlesex, Strawberry Hill, and founded there the Strawberry Hill Press.

Big Brother is watching you
This term is popularly applied to an individual or establishment that exercises dictatorial control, supposedly for everyone's benefit. 'Big Brother' is the invisible state machinery that sees all, from which there is no hiding place, even at home. It is one of the key phrases from George Orwell's (1903–50) *Nineteen Eighty-Four* (1949). Aspects of Orwell's fictional Ministry of Truth were derived not only from the BBC, where he once worked, but also from the experiences of his first wife, Eileen, who worked at the Ministry of Food during the Second World War preparing *Kitchen Front* broadcasts. (See also **Black-coated workers**, q.v.) One campaign to promote potatoes with the slogan 'Potatoes Are Good For You' was so successful that it led to shortages, so it was followed by a 'Potatoes Are Fattening' promotion. In 1984 Orwell was alluding to the Soviet Union of the day, then under Stalin's brutal control; in this country nowadays, however, closed-circuit television has most of our movements covered.

Big enchilada, the
The leader, the top man or woman, the Boss. A phrase that crops up in the Watergate tapes referring to the US Attorney-General, John Mitchell (1913–88), who led President Nixon's re-election campaign in 1972, and who was later indicted on charges that he had conspired to plan the burglary of the Democratic National

Committee's headquarters in the Watergate office-hotel-apartment complex in Washington, DC, and had then obstructed justice and perjured himself during the subsequent cover-up. He was convicted in 1974 and sentenced to a gaol term for 'associated offences' uncovered during the investigation into the scandal. Enchilada is a Mexican speciality, and consists of a tortilla filled with meat and dressed with chilli sauce. It can only be surmised that, since Mexican food is ubiquitous in America, it was the Attorney-General's favourite dish on the hotel menu. Since the mid-1970s, 'the big cheese' is also occasionally used to describe a VIP, especially in business, while a group of them may sometimes be facetiously described as *les grands fromages*. In an echo of Watergate terminology, Monica Lewinsky would sometimes refer to President Clinton as 'the big creep' when she was annoyed with him during their on-off liaison in 1996; by another coincidence, she too lived in the Watergate complex for a time.

Big-stick diplomacy
A political catchphrase which refers to the conduct of negotiations or the carrying out of policy backed up by the threat of military force. The term was brought to public attention in 1901 when US Vice-President Theodore Roosevelt revealed in a speech his fondness for the West African proverb 'Speak softly and carry a big stick'. Later, as President, he used such practices successfully in the Alaskan boundary dispute of 1902–4.

Birds and the bees, the
A euphemism for human procreation which was probably inspired by Cole Porter's 1954 song, 'Let's Do It':

> Birds do it, bees do it
> Even educated fleas do it
> Let's do it, let's fall in love.

The phrase was used, often by embarrassed parents or teachers, as a means of avoiding dangerous words like 'sex' or 'sexual intercourse'; nowadays it tends to be used ironically. In his poem 'Annus Mirabilis' (1967), Philip Larkin (1922–85) wrote that 'Sexual intercourse began in nineteen sixty-three', so in the buttoned-up 1950s roundabout phrases sounding as though they came from the nursery were extremely useful for the unmentionably grown-up subject of sex.

Biscuit – That takes the biscuit
An exclamation to indicate shock and surprise that some action has gone beyond the bounds of acceptable behaviour and implying that the speaker is affronted by this outrageousness. Specially spiced biscuits and cakes were formerly prized as small treats and were given as rewards in a variety of competitions.

Bish-bash-bosh
A Yuppie phrase, mainly current in the 1980s, full of bravado, to describe something done well, quickly and efficiently. It was later shortened to 'bosh' and widely used by manual workers, as if to say, 'Just like that', or 'Sorted'. It gained wide circulation through its use by one of the characters portrayed by the comedian Harry Enfield, the loutish but high-earning plasterer 'Loadsamoney'.

Bishop – As the bishop said to the actress
A rejoinder to a perfectly innocent statement intended to create a sexual *double entendre*, sometimes inverted to become 'As the actress said to the bishop'. Typical comments that might encourage such a retort would be, 'I didn't know I had it in me', or 'I'd bend over backwards to please you', or 'I've never seen a female "Bottom" . . .'. The phrase was popular in the 1940s in the RAF, although it is thought to have originated in the music-hall era, when the staple fare of stand-up comedians included many stories of potentially scandalous couplings between bishops and actresses. In *Educating Archie*, the popular BBC radio

33

show of the 1950s, Beryl Reid as Monica, an upper-class schoolgirl friend of Archie Andrews, the ventriloquist's dummy, used an alternative phrase, '. . . As the art mistress said to the gardener'.

Bitter end, to the
To the last extremity, to the final defeat, or to the death. An affliction can be born until the bitter end, meaning to the last stroke of bad fortune. Despite appearances, the phrase has nothing to do with bitterness. 'Bitter end' is a mid-nineteenth-century nautical term for the end of a rope or chain secured in a vessel's chain locker, or 'abaft the bitts'. When there is no windlass the cables are fastened to bitts, that is, pairs of bollards fixed to the deck, and when the rope is let out until no more remains, the end is at the bitts – hence the bitter end.

In Captain Smith's *Seaman's Grammar* (1627) we read:

> A Bitter is but the turne of a Cable about the Bitts, and vear it out by little and little. And the Bitters end, is that part of the Cable doth stay within boord.

However, the phrase appears in the Old Testament in the context that we use today:

> Her end is bitter as wormwood, sharp as a two-edged sword.
>
> Proverbs 5:4

Black is beautiful
This slogan was adopted in the 1960s by supporters of black civil rights in America in an attempt to destroy the negative associations that the word 'black' had had until then. The West Indian-born civil-rights activist Stokely Carmichael (born Kwame Toure, 1941) coined the phrase in 1966 at a civil-rights rally in Memphis, Tennessee, and Martin Luther King, Jr (1929–68), the leader of the Civil Rights Movement, took it up the following year when he used it in a poster campaign. The expression may have biblical origins:

> I am black, but comely.
>
> Song of Solomon 1:5

Carmichael was the leader of black nationalism in America during the 1960s, and also the originator of its rallying cry, 'Black power'.

Black-coated workers

A euphemism for prunes, in reference to their laxative qualities. The phrase was coined by Charles (later Lord) Hill, the BBC radio doctor in the 1940s, in early-morning radio broadcasts of a programme called *The Kitchen Front* (see **Big Brother is watching you**, q.v.). The expression is a neat counterpoint to the terms 'white-collar workers' – management who sit at desks – and 'blue-collar workers' – the employees in overalls who get their hands dirty. However, the politician and diarist Sir Henry 'Chips' Channon used the phrase literally when writing about the Old-Age Pensions Bill in 1937, referring to those in clerical and professional jobs as 'black-coated workers'.

Blarney Stone, to kiss the

A popular term used of someone who speaks in persuasive or seductive terms; the verb 'to blarney', meaning to employ persuasive flattery, and the noun 'blarney', for flattering talk, have the same derivation. The provenance for this expression can be found, literally, at Blarney Castle, near Cork, in south-west Ireland. Set high in the south wall of the castle is an almost inaccessible triangular stone bearing the inscription, *Cormac Macarthy fortis me fieri fecit*. In 1602, the same Macarthy, Lord of Blarney, was defending the castle against the English, who were fighting to force him to surrender the fortress and transfer his allegiance to the English crown. However, Macarthy smooth-talked the British emissary, Sir George Carew, with flattery and sweet promises and stood his ground, much to the fury of the Queen Elizabeth I; it is said that the Queen herself coined the term 'blarney' to show the worthlessness of Macarthy's promises. The tradition of kissing the Blarney Stone to improve one's eloquence and persuasive abilities – which can only be done by hanging, with one's feet securely held, head-down from the castle's battlements – dates from the eighteenth century. 'To blarney' is also a slang American term meaning to pick locks.

Blood, sweat and tears

The phrase comes from Winston Churchill's speech to the House of Commons upon taking over as Prime Minister, 13 May 1940, and is used to describe a task that will be hard and difficult, demanding great sacrifice with few if any compensations. At the time British morale was at a low ebb: Nazi forces had overrun Denmark, Holland and Belgium, and were in the process of conquering Norway and France. The prospect of victory over Germany looked increasingly grim. Churchill's actual words were, 'I have nothing to offer but blood, toil, tears and sweat,' and he revisited this phrase several times during the war years. It has since been reduced to just three words, making it easier to remember, without losing any of its emphatic meaning of selfless hard work and dedication.

Some three centuries earlier, John Donne (c. 1572–1631) wrote in 'An Anatomy of the World' (1611):

Mollify it with thy tears, or sweat, or blood.

While Lord Byron (1788–1824) observed in *The Age of Bronze* (1823):

Year after year they voted cent per cent,
Blood, sweat and tear wrung millions – why? For the rent!

In 1882 the Italian patriot Giuseppe Garibaldi (1807–82) made this speech to his followers in the struggle for Italian nationhood, which may well have inspired Churchill:

Soldiers, I'm getting out of Rome. Anyone who wants to carry on the war against the outsiders, come with me. I can't offer you either honours nor wages, I offer you hunger, thirst, forced marches, battles and death. Anyone who loves his country, follow me.

Blood Sweat and Tears was also the name of an American jazz/rock band in the 1960s and 1970s.

Blow hot and cold, to

To be inconsistent, to have fluctuating opinions, or simply to be unable to make up one's mind. The allusion is to the classical fable of a traveller who accepted the hospitality of a satyr, one of the gods of the forest, a creature part goat and part man. The chilly traveller blew on his cold fingers to warm them and then blew on his hot broth to cool it. The indignant satyr ejected him because he blew both hot and cold with the same breath.

Blow the gaff
A slang phrase meaning to reveal a secret, which may derive from French *gaffe*, a blunder, but it is more likely to come from 'gab', the informal English word for speech, which in turn derives from 'gob', meaning mouth or beak (the expression 'gift of the gab' comes from the same source). Current in the eighteenth century was a slang expression, 'to blow the gab', meaning to betray a secret. A more colourful derivation, however, may be that the phrase refers to a concealed device, known as a gaff, used to cheat at cards. This was a small hook set in a ring worn on the finger and used by the crooked player to grip the cards. In America and Canada, the expression 'to stand the gaff' means to withstand problems, scorn and other troubles. 'Gaff' is also archaic English slang for someone's home, as in 'Let's go round to his gaff'.

Blue-rinse brigade, the
Although this phrase has a military ring, it is used to describe women of a certain age with conservative tendencies. It is a slightly derogatory description that refers to the colour of the rinse used to conceal grey hair; conveniently, blue is the Conservative Party colour. The collective term 'brigade' was obviously applied because of the formidable presence these ladies make at political meetings, party conferences and other rallies of the faithful, but the term can be extended to encompass any group of well-groomed, socially active, usually well-off, elderly women.

Bogart – Don't Bogart that joint
A widely used phrase that comes from the film *Easy Rider* (1969), which featured a song by Holy Modal Rounders called 'Don't Bogart That Joint'. It means to take too long to pass the joint, or cannabis cigarette, to the next person. The term 'to bogart' was obviously inspired by the film actor Humphrey Bogart (1899–1957), who more often than not appeared on screen as well as in

public with a cigarette hanging from his lip; perhaps unsurprisingly, he died from lung cancer.

Bone to pick, to have a
This is a desire to discuss a difference of opinion, settle a misunderstanding about something disagreeable, or express a complaint. The bone is probably the bone of contention, metaphorically tossed between two dogs fighting over it. Usage goes back to the middle of the sixteenth century, but the expression may well have come from an earlier phrase, 'to have a crow to pluck', which was used at least a hundred years earlier, the crow in this instance symbolizing discord. In Howell's *Proverbs* (1659) the phrase 'to have a goose to pluck with you' is used in the same sense.

Bone up on, to
To study intensively, to engage in serious research into a particular subject, or to revise a subject comprehensively. It has been said 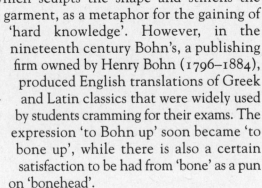 that the allusion is to whalebone in a corset, which sculpts the shape and stiffens the garment, as a metaphor for the gaining of 'hard knowledge'. However, in the nineteenth century Bohn's, a publishing firm owned by Henry Bohn (1796–1884), produced English translations of Greek and Latin classics that were widely used by students cramming for their exams. The expression 'to Bohn up' soon became 'to bone up', while there is also a certain satisfaction to be had from 'bone' as a pun on 'bonehead'.

Bones, to make no
To be honest and direct without any risk that the statement may be misunderstood, but also sometimes used to mean to have no scruples about something. A possible derivation for this phrase is that it comes from the world of gambling, a pursuit that has been popular since the eighteenth century. Dice were often known as

'bones', perhaps because in play they are rattled together and sound like castanets, which in turn used to be known as bones (from which they were made). Once dice have been thrown the score is a gamble; therefore if you make no bones, you will incur no risk – a situation that cannot be misinterpreted. Dice are said to have been invented in China by Chen Su-Wang in the third century AD, so the phrase may well have been in use for hundreds of years. Another derivation, however, suggests a reference to the simple pleasure of drinking a bowl of soup in which there are no bones, and thus nothing to complain about.

Born-again Christian

A person who has undergone a spiritual conversion and become a fervent and sometimes evangelizing Christian; by extension, 'born-again' is now used of anyone newly converted to some activity or cause, as in 'born-again Socialist'. The phrase was originally applied to fundamentalist Christians in the Southern United States and has been in use since at least the 1960s, although the term originates in the New Testament with the story of Christ and Nicodemus (John 3: 3):

> Except a man be born again, he cannot see the kingdom of God.

Originally the phrase took on a figurative meaning of zealousness, and especially the zealousness of the newly converted, at about the time when Jimmy Carter, from a born-again Baptist background in the South, was running for the American presidency in 1976. The epithet 'born-again' is usually, but not necessarily, religious. A born-again golfer is one who, having played golf occasionally over the years, becomes a regular player on retirement. Currently, with divorce becoming relatively common, many ex-wives describe themselves, somewhat profanely, as 'a born-again virgin'.

Bottom line, the

The main point of an argument, the basic characteristic of something or the actual value of a financial deal, the nub or truth of the matter. The phrase gained wide currency during the 1970s possibly, because of its frequent use by the US Secretary of State,

Henry Kissinger. He spoke of 'the bottom line' as the eventual outcome of a negotiation – ignoring the distraction of any inessential detail. The phrase itself is an accounting term, and refers to the figure on the line at the end of a financial statement indicating the net profit or loss of a company.

Break a leg!

The theatre is notoriously superstitious, and among actors it is deemed bad luck to wish a colleague 'good luck' before going on stage. Instead, this phrase, a traditional, if somewhat black, euphemism, is employed to wish someone good luck in a performance, especially on a first night. The expression, which seems to have originated in America, is said to come from the assassination of President Abraham Lincoln in his private box at Ford's Theatre, Washington, DC, on 14 April 1865. The murderer, John Wilkes Booth, a reputable Shakespearian actor, escaped after firing the shot by leaping down on to the stage, breaking his leg in the process. 'Break a leg!' may derive from a German expression for good luck, *Hals und Beinbruch* ('May you break your neck and your leg'), with which the Kaiser's pilots used to wish each other luck during the First World War.

Breakfast of Champions, the

An American advertising slogan associated since the 1950s with Wheaties, whose television commercials featured sporting champions endorsing the cereal. In what is known as a chiastic twist, this phrase can also be inverted to read, 'The champion of breakfasts'. Perhaps in acknowledgement of the slogan's success, Kurt Vonnegut (1922–) published a novel entitled *The Breakfast of Champions* in 1973.

Bridesmaid – Always a bridesmaid, never a bride

The phrase actually originated as 'Often a bridesmaid . . .', and was coined to advertise Listerine mouthwash in 1923. It was created by Milton Feasley of the advertising agency Lambert & Feasley, although it is reminiscent of the British music-hall song 'Why Am I Always a Bridesmaid?' made famous by Lily Morris. A screen title in the newsreel sequence of Orson Welles's film *Citizen Kane* (1941) proclaims of Kane, 'In politics, always a bridesmaid never a bride'. The bridesmaid advertisement was succeeded by an even more famous line used to promote Listerine: 'Even your best friends won't tell you . . .' (that is, that your breath smells).

Bright young things

A typically sparkling phrase invented by the prolific romantic novelist and former journalist Barbara Cartland (1902–2000) to describe the young socialites of the years following the First World War. As a counterpoint to the horrors of war it was all the rage to dance the night away in a riot of frivolous partying, possibly in a subconscious attempt to deny that the war had ever happened, or at least to try to forget the bloody conflict. In the 1920s young women in their teens, and especially those who were unconventional in their dress, manner or behaviour, were known as 'flappers' – many of them wore their hair in a plait tied with a bow, which flapped when they danced. They came to epitomize the meaning of the phrase 'Bright young things'.

Buck – The buck stops here

A slightly self-important declaration meaning 'This is where ultimate responsibility lies'. 'Buck' is slang for the American and Canadian dollars, and possibly derives from deer hunting, the bucks (males) being more valuable than the does (females). As well as being a male deer, hare or rat (among other animals), a high-spirited young man, a young dandy or, in a more derogatory sense, a male Native American or African-American, a 'buck' is also an article placed as a reminder before a player whose turn it is

41

to deal at poker, and it is very likely that the slogan actually originated at the poker table (see next entry), and has nothing to do with dollars. The phrase was made famous by US President Harry S Truman (1884–1972; President 1945–53), who had it hand-written on a sign on his desk at the White House to remind himself and those around him that he alone had the ultimate responsibility for every decision of his administration. Some twenty-five years later President Jimmy Carter had the legend reinstated with the same idea in mind. In a perceived lowering of public respect for the morals of certain American presidents, however, the phrase was later modified in common usage to 'The f**k stops here' (see also **The big enchilada**, q.v.). The original phrase is now generally applied to the boss of any organization.

Buck – To pass the buck
To evade blame or responsibility and shift all criticism elsewhere. An American phrase from the game of poker, the 'buck' being the token object that is passed to the person who wins a jackpot, to remind him that when it is his turn to deal the next hand he must start another jackpot. Originally the token was a buckhorn knife, so called because its handle was made from the horn of a buck, or male deer; although some sources argue that the buck was either a piece of buckshot or a buck's tail, which early hunters carried as a lucky talisman. The earliest recorded use of the phrase is by Mark Twain (born Samuel Langhorn Clemens; 1835–1910) in 1872, in the first decade after the end of the Civil War, when poker or 'stud poker' – the stake was probably originally a stud horse – were played in bars by lumberjacks, miners and hunters, those being the days before it became known as a 'gentleman's' game. (See also entry above.)

Bullet – To bite the bullet
To seize the moment when one undertakes a feat of endurance, to face danger with courage and fortitude, to behave stoically, to knuckle down to some difficult or unpleasant task. The expression probably originated in field surgery before the use of anaesthetics. A surgeon about to operate on a wounded soldier would give him a bullet to bite on, both to distract him from the pain and to reduce his ability to scream.

Business as usual

This self-explanatory expression was widely used in Britain in the Second World War, and especially during the London Blitz and the blitzes on other major cities, when shops and businesses continued to open, and stay open, in spite of bomb damage. In the capital, 'Business as usual' and 'London can take' it were commonly scrawled defiantly on the walls of damaged buildings. Winston Churchill popularized the phrase in 1941 in a speech at the Guild Hall in London when he said, 'The maxim of the British people is "Business as usual".' A later Conservative Prime Minister, Margaret (now Lady) Thatcher, memorably evoked the fighting spirit behind these words after the IRA bomb attack on the Grand Hotel in Brighton during the Conservative Party Conference of 1984.

By a long chalk

This expression comes from the athletics or sports arena, and means to win easily, far ahead of the competition. The allusion is probably to chalk marks made on the floor to record the score of a player of team, and the phrase sounds as if it originated with the long jump or throwing the javelin, or some sport of that nature where the greatest distance determines the winner. Before lead pencils became common, merit marks or scores used to be made with chalk. A long chalk, therefore, is a high score.

C'est la guerre

An ironic phrase employed to accompany an excuse or an explanation for anything that has not gone quite to plan. Originally a French military catchphrase from the First World War, it was used as a somewhat fatalistic excuse for any failure to perform properly. By 1915 it had been taken up by British soldiers, although after the Armistice its use declined until its revival in the next war. It was then widely used in a civilian, as well as a military, context to account for anything that had been affected as result of the war. It is nowadays used, especially in business, to indicate acceptance of matters beyond one's control, and naturally prompts the use of the similar phrase of gritty acceptance, *C'est la vie* ('That's life').

Camp – As camp as a row of tents

An expression used to describe something – a man, a theatre performance, an outfit, and so on – that is blatantly homosexual or wildly and effeminately affected, especially anything that is in questionable taste. The phrase, which is sometimes seen as 'As camp as a row of little pink tents', is a pun on the double meaning of the word camp and is a variation on other euphemisms for homosexual, like 'As bent as a lighthouse staircase' or 'As queer as a nine-bob note'. The adjective 'camp' does not necessarily mean homosexual, although it invariably has those overtones; it also carries with it a strong hint of self-parody. The colour pink may be associated with gay men because in Hitler's Germany known homosexuals were forced by the Nazis to wear a triangle of pink cloth as a means of identification. The spending power of gays, especially in an area, like London's Soho, where there is a substantial gay community, is called the 'economy of the pink pound'.

Cards – To ask for (or be given) one's cards

To ask for or be given one's cards is to resign from or be dismissed from a job. The cards in question are the National Insurance cards and other documents kept by the employer as a record of income tax and insurance contributions deducted from an employee's pay. In a sporting extension of this phrase, if a player, particularly in football, is shown a card by the referee, he is in breach of the rules; a yellow card represents a warning and red card means the player is sent off the field.

Carpe diem

Do not put off until tomorrow what can be done today, or enjoy the present while you have the chance. This has been for centuries a popular poetic theme or motif, urging the young to grasp the joys of life, especially love, before it is too late. The phrase is Latin for 'seize the day' and probably first appeared in literature in the first century BC; the Roman poet Horace (Quintus Horatius Flaccus, 65 BC–8 BC) wrote in his *Odes* (*c*. 23–13 BC):

Carpe diem, quam minimum credula posterio.
Seize the day, put no trust in the future.

The same spirited call to enjoy the pleasures of life was expressed by many later poets, among them Robert Herrick (1591–1674), whose 'To the Virgins, to Make Much of Time' (1648) enjoins maidens to abandon their virginity and live life to the full:.

Gather ye rosebuds while ye may,
Old Time is still a-flying:
And this same flower that smiles today,
Tomorrow will be dying.

Saul Bellow's (1915–) novella *Seize the Day* (1956) treats the theme ironically, portraying the effects of failure to follow one's authentic impulses. The phrase gained increased popularity after the Oscar-winning film *Dead Poets Society* (1989), directed by Peter Weir and starring Robin Williams as the passionate and inspiring teacher John Keating, who calls to his class, '*Carpe diem*, lads. Seize the day. Make your lives extraordinary!' Nowadays, the expression is often used of any opportunity that should be seized before it is too late.

Case the joint, to

An American slang expression from the criminal fraternity meaning to inspect or reconnoitre a building carefully before attempting to rob it, or to break into it for some other nefarious purpose. 'Joint' in this context means a building, an early twentieth-century colloquial Americanism for a sleazy dive where opium could be smoked or, during the Prohibition era (1920–33), where illicit spirits could be bought and drunk. National prohibition, which resulted from the Eighteenth Amendment to the US Constitution forbidding the manufacture, sale, transportation and consumption of alcoholic beverages, was known – by its supporters, at least – as 'the Noble Experiment', prohibitionists believing that alcohol was a dangerous drug that destroyed lives and communities. In the event, however, illegal trading in alcohol made many fortunes, and gave a tremendous boost to organized crime. The word 'joint' has since come to be generally applied disparagingly to almost any more or less disreputable establishment, especially less than salubrious public meeting places like certain clubs, pubs or restaurants.

Cast pearls before swine, to
To offer something precious or of quality to someone who is perceived to be too ignorant or uncultured to understand or appreciate it. To show, for example, a brilliant idea or a work of art or literature to, or to bring one's 'pearls of wisdom' before, an unappreciative audience or the kind of person known as a Philistine. Philistines were warlike immigrants to Philistia in ancient Palestine, who fought the Israelites for possession of the land, and hence came to be stigmatized as an uneducated, heathen enemy; the term has since by extension come to mean anyone unreceptive or hostile to culture, especially someone who is smugly and boorishly so.

The phrase itself comes from the New Testament (Matthew 7: 6):

> Give not that which is holy unto the dogs, neither cast ye your pearls before swine, lest they trample them under their feet.

Cat – All cats love fish but fear to wet their paws
A traditional saying, dating back to at least the sixteenth century, used to describe a person who is keen to obtain something of value, but who is not bold enough to make the necessary effort or to take the risk. It is to this saying that Shakespeare referred in *Macbeth*:

Letting 'I dare not' wait upon 'I would',
Like the poor cat i' the adage.

Cat – No room to swing a cat
A commonly used description for a restricted or cramped space.
There are various suggested origins for this phrase, of which the most
likely is not as cruel to cats as it sounds, but was not much fun for the
metaphorical cat's human victim. 'Cat' was an abbreviation for 'cat-
o'-nine tails', a whip of nine knotted lashes or 'tails' which from the
eighteenth century was used in the army and navy, as well as on criminals in gaol, and was not formally banned in England as an instrument of punishment until 1948. It was a popularly held superstition
that lashing with a 'trinity of trinities', that is nine, was a a more effec-
tive punishment. Since space was restricted on the old sailing ships, it
may be that it was the amount of elbow room available that determined when the cat was swung. However, while this may seem the
most likely origin, 'cat' is also an old Scottish word for a rogue, and if
the expression derives from this, the swing is that of the condemned
criminal hanging from the gallows. Equally, suspending live cats in
leather sacks and then swinging the sacks as moving targets for
archers was once a popular, if barbaric, amusement, and this too has
been suggested as a source for the phrase.

Cat – The cat's pyjamas
This colloquialism first surfaced in
America in the 1900s and has
retained its meaning over the last
hundred years. It became current in
England in the 1920s and 1930s as a
phrase meaning something or some-
one superlatively good, top-notch or
extremely enticing, the last perhaps because of some saucy link
between pyjamas and bedtime.

'The cat's whiskers' and 'the bee's knees' are also used in the
same way. In the first crystal wireless sets of the 1920s, the fine
wire that made contact with the crystal was known as the cat's
whisker, alluding to the sensitivity of cats' whiskers. At about the
same time, people played with phrases that linked animals to

humans, and we find 'the kipper's knickers', 'the snake's hips', 'the elephant's instep' and so on. However, in the last ten years modern imagination has taken the idea further, and we now have more ribald phrases such as 'the dog's bollocks', which is sometimes abbreviated to just 'the dog's'.

Cat – To fight like Kilkenny cats

This is a fight to the end, no holds (as in wrestling) barred. The connection between fighting and Kilkenny cats is obscure. From the Norman period until 1843, Kilkenny was divided into Englishtown and Irishtown, with much strife between the two. One theory harks back to a legendary battle between a thousand cats from Kilkenny and a thousand cats from other parts of Ireland. In the night-long battle all the Kilkenny cats survived victorious, while all the others perished. Another more popular theory dates fom about 1800, when Kilkenny was occupied by a group of Hessian mercenaries in British government service, some of whom, bored and with nothing better to do, tied two cats to a clothes line by their tails and sat back to enjoy the feline fight. The soldiers had no time to release the cats when an officer approached to investigate the noise, so they cut the animals free by severing their tails. The officer was told that the cats had fought so fiercely that only their tails remained.

Catch-22, a Catch-22 situation

This is a lose-lose situation; whichever alternative you choose you can't win. It is the title of former advertising copywriter Joseph Heller's (1923–99) highly regarded satirical novel published in 1955. The story centres on Captain Yossarian of the 256th US Army Air Force bombing squadron in the Second World War, whose main aim in life is to avoid being killed. The best way for a pilot to achieve this was to be grounded due to insanity.

> There was only one catch and that was Catch-22 which specified that concern for one's own safety in the face of dangers that were real and immediate was the process of a rational mind. Orr was crazy and could be grounded. All he had to do was to ask and as soon as he did he would no longer be crazy and would have to fly more missions.

Century of the common man, the

The twentieth century is known as 'the century of the common man', the age of democracy. The phrase comes from the 1940 book of the same name by Henry A Wallace (1888–1965), New Dealer and FD Roosevelt's Vice-President, 1940–45. He subsequently used the phrase after America had joined the Allied forces in the Second World War, in an address entitled 'The Price of Free World Victory' on 8 May 1942:

> The century in which we are entering – the century which will come out of this war – can be and must be the century of the common man.

The phrase speedily became popular on both sides of the Atlantic and was much favoured by Nancy, Viscountess Astor (1879–1964), outspoken Conservative and, although American born, first woman MP to sit in the House of Commons, which she did from 1919 to 1945. In the late 1930s, she supported an appeasement policy toward Nazi Germany. When Britain declared war, however, she strongly supported the war effort.

The American composer, and prominent champion of American music, Aaron Copland, appropriately born in 1900, wrote *Fanfare for the Common Man*.

Changes, to ring the

This phrase is often used incorrectly as meaning to make changes. It actually means to repeat the same thing in a different way, and comes from the world of bell ringing, which was at its most popular in Britain in the seventeenth century. A change is the order in which a series of bells is rung. Thus with a series of four bells, as in the Westminster chimes, it is possible to ring twenty-four changes without once repeating the order in which the bells are struck. With five bells 120 changes can be rung, and with twelve bells 479,001,600 are possible. The greatest number of changes ever actually rung is reported to have been 16,000 changes, which took about nine hours. Someone who repeats the same statement or idea, *ad nauseam* and with only minor variations, rings 'all' the changes.

Charity begins at home

This old proverb, meaning 'look to yourself and those close to you before helping others', is listed in the *Concise Oxford Dictionary of Proverbs*, which dates it from 1383, although it has a biblical counterpart:

> But if any widow have children or nephews let them learn first to shew piety at home.
>
> 1 Timothy 5:4

Writers have played with it ever since; for instance, in 1732 Fuller wrote, 'Charity begins at home, but should not end there', and Charles Dickens in *Martin Chuzzlewit* has, 'Charity begins at home and justice begins next door.' Other cultures have sayings alluding to acts of charity, one Russian proverb advising, 'Don't collect straw for your neighbour's roof while your own is leaking'.

Charlie's dead

A slang euphemism used to indicate that a woman's petticoat is showing, or that a trouser zip is undone. This expression has been in use since the 1950s, though the origin and identity of Charlie can only be guessed at. 'Charlie' is English slang for a fool and may come from Cockney rhyming slang for Charlie Hunt (i.e. c**t), used euphemistically, as 'Charlie's come', to describe anything that is unmentionable or unwelcome, such as the onset of menstruation. In Australian rhyming slang a Charlie is a girl, derived from Charlie Wheeler – 'sheila'.

Chattering classes, the

A wry description of journalists, political pundits and the like, members of the so-called 'classless society', who discuss current affairs and social issues. More generally, this is a slightly derogatory term for groups of would-be or pseudo-intellectuals pontificating on subjects of which they have perhaps incomplete knowledge, and certainly no control. Such types used to be called 'armchair philosophers'. The term was first coined some twenty years ago, at

the beginning of Margaret Thatcher's reign as Prime Minister, as a disparaging description of the liberal middle classes who impotently raged against Thatcherite policies around the dinner tables of London.

Cheque-book journalism
A phrase first heard in the mid-1960s to describe the activities of the highly competitive press when trying to secure exclusive rights to stories from notorious personalities and criminals, in the latter case sending out a rather misleading message that crime does pay. Sex scandals, for instance, known as 'kiss-and-tell' stories, involve scorned ex-partners being tempted by the tabloid press, particularly, to sell their salacious accounts. The freedom of the press is a highly valued privilege in Britain and there remains a fierce debate about the ethics of paying for lurid stories, however colourful, the invasion of privacy being set against the press's need to provide the public with what they want to read.

Chickens – Don't count your chickens until they are hatched
To assume something is certain before it is proved to be so. It is well known that, in modern parlance, 'assumption is the mother of all f**k ups', and it is wise to heed this when planning ahead. The phrase has certainly been around for thousands of years, since it appears in Aesop's fable of the 'Milkmaid and Her Pail'. Indeed, there are probably more versions of this proverb than any other.

> The man that once did sell the lion's skin
> While the beast liv'd, was kill'd with hunting him,

wrote Shakespeare in Henry V, while a Hindu proverb urges, 'Don't bargain for fish which are still in the water', and an ancient Egyptian saw cautions, 'Do not rejoice over what has not yet happened'. A colloquial modern alternative from the betting shop is, 'Don't count your winnings until the bookie has put the money in your hand.'

Chip on one's shoulder, to have a

To display an inferiority complex, to perceive oneself as an underdog, to have a grievance, often unjustifiably. The expression is believed to have originated in America in about 1840 and may allude to a game of dare in which a man challenges another to dislodge a chip – as in piece of wood, not French fry – he carries on his shoulder. In American parlance a chip was also a figurative term for consequences, and so the phrase may be a warning to an adversary not to aim too high. There is an ancient proverb 'Hew not too high lest chips fall in thine eye'. By the late sixteenth century this health-and-safety warning had become something of a challenge, a dare to a fearless woodcutter to look high up without regard to any falling chips of wood.

Chips with everything

This comes from the days when Britain was over-concerned with social class, and is a snobbish comment on the perceived less adventurous appetites of the working classes. It implies a British taste for everything to be served with chips, usually drenched in vinegar or ketchup, and neatly describes the sort of British tourist who travels abroad and demands chips with everything, from pizza to curry. In 1962 Arnold Wesker (1932–) wrote a play entitled *Chips With Everything* about class attitudes among National Servicemen in the RAF. Nowadays, the phrase takes on a slightly different meaning with the increasing significance of computer chips in our lives.

Chuck out your chintz

A catchy alliterative phrase used by the Swedish-owned chain Ikea in 1999 to persuade people to buy new furniture from their stores. Chintz is a hybrid word, first heard in Britain in the seventeenth century when cotton fabric with floral designs was imported from the East. The Hindi word *chint* means variegated. The many chint fabrics soon became chints, and, in time the spelling was changed to chintz.

Clean, bright and lightly oiled

This is an army slogan that goes back to the First World War, and describes the approved state for a soldier's rifle. Between the wars, 'slightly oiled' came to mean to be a bit tipsy, alluding to the property of oil as a lubricant. By the same token, 'well oiled' means drunk. In the next war, the phrase took on military connotations again, and Gerald Kersh used it as the title of a book of wartime short stories in 1946.

Cleanliness is next to godliness

This homely phrase comes from a sermon given by John Wesley in a sermon in 1791, although it is thought to have its origins in the writings of an ancient Hebrew rabbi, Phinehas ben Yair. A British advertising agent, Thomas J Barratt (1842–1914), seeking an endorsement for Pears Soap in America in the 1880s, was naturally shy of approaching former President Grant and instead asked the eminent American cleric, Henry Ward Beecher, to say a few kind words about his product. Beecher wrote a text including the phrase, which entered the lexicon of English both as an unforgettable advertising strap-line and as a moral statement or injunction.

Clean round the bend

Completely crazy, eccentric, in the sense of being out of alignment. The phrase was described by FC Bowen in the *Oxford English Dictionary* in 1929 as 'an old naval term for anybody who is mad'. The word 'clean' is used in many different ways to describe something complete, pure, or unreserved, for instance 'clean bowled', 'to make a clean break' or 'to make a clean breast of it'. In a neat play on words the phrase has been used to advertise the lavatory cleaner Harpic since the 1930s – 'It cleans right round the bend'.

Clear the decks, to

To remove everything not required, especially when preparing for action; hence, to prepare for some task by removing the extraneous or irrelevant. As it sounds, this is a nautical phrase and alludes to a sailing ship preparing for battle, when anything in the way of the guns and their crews, or that might burn or splinter, or that was not lashed down, was removed from the usually cluttered decks, so that no untethered articles would roll about and injure the seamen during the battle. This saying is used in many contexts, such as clearing the table of food and dishes, or preparing the house to receive guests. 'Deck' appears in many commonly used phrases, among them 'to hit the deck', to fall over, usually to escape injury, or 'to deck someone', to hit them and knock them to the floor.

Cleft stick, to be in a

A figurative phrase meaning to be in a tight place or dilemma, with no room for manoeuvre either backwards nor forwards. The phrase may be an ancient pun on the verb 'to cleave' which has two directly opposite meanings, one being to stick to or adhere, and the other to split, chop or break along a grain or line of cleavage.

The form of torture inflicted on Ariel by the witch Sycorax in Shakespeare's *The Tempest* (1611) was to imprison him in the trunk of a cleft pine tree.

Cloak and dagger
Any operation that involves some intrigue, especially the melodramatic undercover activities of those involved in espionage or other secret work. Cloak-and-dagger plays were swashbuckling adventures popular in the seventeenth century. In France a performance of this type was known as a *comédie de cape et d'épée* and this is the direct source of the English phrase, 'cloak and dagger'. The name also appears in the Spanish *comedias de capa y espaded*, literally comedies of cloak and sword, particularly those by the Spanish dramatists Lope de Vega (1562–1635) and Calderón (1600–81), although these plays were dramas of merely domestic intrigue.

Clockwork orange
A person who has been brainwashed to alter his or her personality, particularly someone whose individuality has been suppressed by conditioning. The term comes from the title of the novel *A Clockwork Orange* (1962) by Anthony Burgess (1917–93) which was popularized by Stanley Kubrick's controversial and violent film of the same title (1971). The story tells of the state's attempts to punish its criminal hero, Alex, by turning him into a 'mechanical man' through sinister forms of therapy and brainwashing. In spite of its success the film was taken out of circulation by Kubrick and Warner Brothers after it was blamed for a number of copycat crimes as reported by the police and the courts; Kubrick himself also received several death threats. Following the director's death in 1999 the film was re-released in 2000. Burgess took his title from a little known Cockney expression from the 1950s, 'as queer as a clockwork orange', that is, homosexual, which may derive from the phrase 'as odd as an orange'.

Closet, to come out of the
To declare one's homosexuality, to come out into the open about it. This was the slogan of the American gay rights organization known

as the Gay Liberation Front from about 1969. In the days when homosexuality was a criminal offence, gay men had to hide the nature of their sexual preferences. (Lesbianism has never been criminalized in Britain, since at the time the legislation was formulated Queen Victoria refused to believe that sexual relations between women could ever occur.) They became known as closet queens, the closet being a private room; closet plays, for instance, are written to be read, not acted. When anti-homosexual laws were repealed, the need for secrecy receded and gays were able 'to come out', although many, fearful of society's disapproval, remained 'in the closet'. The expression is now used generally to mean to declare one's real position. The phrase 'to come out' was used in the first half of the twentieth century of debutantes, upper-class young women who were presented at Court, so making their official debut in society.

Cloud nine, on

To be on cloud nine means to be in a state of elation, very happy indeed, or feeling 'as high as a kite'. This fanciful twentieth-century expression comes from the terminology used by the United States Weather Bureau. The Bureau divides clouds into classes, and each class into nine types. Cloud nine is cumulonimbus, a cumulus cloud that develops to a vast height, with rounded masses of white vapour heaped one on the other, the upper parts resembling the shapes of domes, mountains or towers, while the base is practically horizontal.

Coat – To cut your coat according to your cloth
This metaphorical proverb is all about good
housekeeping and living within one's means.
It is self-evidently sensible advice to keep
to one's budget and restrict expenditure
to the amount of one's income; in
other words, simply to live within
one's means. It is often shortened,
becoming simply 'to cut your coat'.

Cock-and-bull story
A rambling or incredible tale; a tall story invented as an excuse; a
lie. There are various possible explanations for the derivation for
this term. In the coaching days of the seventeenth century the
London coach changed horses at the Bull Inn and the Birmingham
coach at the Cock Inn. From the exchange of travellers' stories
and jokes between the waiting passengers of both coaches the
'Cock-and-Bull' story is said to have originated.

The phrase may derive, however, from ancient fables in which
cocks and bulls and other animals conversed. In his Boyle Lecture
of 1692, Richard Bentley (1662–1742) stated:

> That cocks and bulls might discourse, and hinds and panthers hold
> conferences about religion.

While in his novel *Tristram Shandy* (1759–67) Laurence Sterne
(1713–68) wrote:

> 'L—d! said my mother, what is all this story about?
> 'A Cock and Bull,' said Yorick – 'And one of the best of its kind,
> I have ever heard.'

A Scottish satire or lampooning story is known as a 'cockalane',
which is taken directly from the French phrase of the same
meaning as 'cock and bull', *coq et l'âne*, cock and ass, donkey or
fool. Today both words are commonly employed separately in a
slang or vulgar context. 'Bull' is used as in 'What a load of bull',
politely avoiding saying the word 'bullshit' – while 'cock' speaks
for itself.

Cold enough to freeze the balls off a brass monkey

This means that the weather is extremely cold, and although the expression sounds delightfully vulgar, it is not in fact a reference to monkeys' testicles. A brass monkey is a type of rack in which cannon balls were stored. Being brass, the 'monkey' contracted in cold weather, resulting in the cannonballs being ejected. The expression has also mutated to a shortened form, again a comment on the temperature, as 'brass-monkey weather', which is almost universally understood.

Come up and see me sometime

This sexy phrase was immortalized by Hollywood screen actress and siren, Mae West (1892–1980). The line first appeared in the play *Diamond Lil* (1928), but probably reached a wider audience in the film version, *She Done Him Wrong* (1933), in which Mae West played a saloonkeeper who falls for the young Cary Grant's undercover cop. In one scene she says to Grant:

> You know, I always did like a man in uniform. And that one fits you grand. Why don't you come up sometime and see me? I'm home every evening.

The original order of the words has been rearranged to make them easier to say, and subsequently this is how WC Fields quotes them to Mae West in *My Little Chickadee* (1939). The American author Gelett Burgess (1866–1951) is credited as the originator of the phrase in his 1907 book *Are You a Bromide?*

Corridors of power, the

A collective expression to describe the ministries in Whitehall and their high-powered civil servants. The phrase was first coined by CP Snow (1905–80) in his novel *Homecomings* (1956):

The official world, the corridors of power, the dilemmas of conscience and egotism – she disliked them all.

Snow later used it as the title of his 1964 novel, and the phrase quickly caught on with the public and newspaper-headline writers.

Couch potato

American slang from about the late 1980s, used to describe a 'telly addict', someone who indulges in the habit of lounging at home watching television all day and night, eating and drinking, but never taking exercise. The expression is now used in most English-speaking countries, particularly with the increase in the number of television channels to choose from. Perhaps the potato featured in the metaphor because the blemishes on its skin are known as eyes, or possibly because it is the tuber of the potato plant, thus punning with 'the tube' – the television. Couch potatoes indulging in the habit of 'channel hopping' use the remote control or 'zapper', in many homes affectionately known by the name of 'Frank' after the zany pop artist Frank Zappa.

Coughs and sneezes spread diseases

A public-health slogan proclaimed by the Ministry of Health during the early days of the Second World War, in an effort to reduce the number of working days lost by workers taking sick leave for minor ailments.

This was a zealous campaign to persuade people not to sneeze in close proximity to each other, especially on public transport and in air-raid shelters, and the phrase is still used today. Tony Hancock, in his classic *Hancock's Half Hour* episode, 'The Blood Donor', reads the health poster bearing this legend while he waits to give his 'armful' of blood. The sister slogan was 'Trap germs in your handkerchief'.

Crazy mixed-up kid
An American term for the first post-Second World War generation of teenagers. Without the pressures of war, many teenagers found they could relax and turn their backs on responsibility, sometimes pretending to suffer from post-war trauma, or otherwise showing such symptoms as confusion, inability to make moral distinctions, and occasionally displaying mild psychological traits. Some argue that many of these went on to become hippies, although it is more likely that they have settled down and are now running the country.

Credibility gap
The space between the truth and fantasy; the disparity that exists between a claim or statement on one hand, and the reality of the situation on the other. If such claims are repeated it naturally results in a loss of confidence in those making such exaggerations. The phrase is generally attributed to Gerald Ford in 1966, while he was still a US Congressman, referring to the escalating involvement of America in the Vietnam War, an assertion that was strongly disputed by Lyndon Johnson's administration. Modern office jargon has bred a new buzz phrase, 'gap analysis', which means the assessment of untapped business opportunities.

Cropper, to come a
To fall heavily, head over heels, or to fail ignominiously. The origin probably lies in the old barber's term for a short haircut, 'neck and crop', which came to be used colloquially to mean headlong or bodily. So to fall to the ground neck and crop is to 'come a cropper', a phrase which has distinctly Cockney overtones with its alliteration and abbreviation.

Cross my heart
To make a firm promise or a pledge that will not be broken, with religious overtones. The words are often accompanied by a sign of the cross made over the heart, and to emphasize the seriousness of

the pledge to add a note of mortality, as quoted in Rose Macaulay's *Crewe Train* (1926):

> Let's both swear,
> Cross my heart and hope to die.

Curate's egg, the

This phrase is one of many from Mr Punch and it is one his most famous punch lines (see **as pleased as Punch,** q.v.). 'Good in parts, like the curate's egg' is proverbial. An elaborate cartoon from 1895 shows a timid young curate at his bishop's breakfast table, too nervous to say that the egg is bad. The phrase is often misquoted to mean that some parts of a thing are good. In fact, the curate was too shy to tell the bishop the truth about the egg.

> I'm afraid you've got a bad egg, Mr Jones.

To which the curate stammers, 'Oh, no my Lord, I assure you! Parts of it are excellent!'

Curse of *Hello!*, the

The popular magazine *Hello!* features glowing and obsequiously uncritical celebrations of the lifestyles of the rich and famous. It has been noticed that some of the happy couples who appear on the front cover do not remain so for many months to follow. Such couples whose marriages have run into trouble include the Duke and Duchess of York and Mr and Mrs Paul Gascoigne. The phrase was probably invented by the satirical magazine *Private Eye*, deriving from its irreverent column, 'The Curse of Gnome'.

Customer – The customer is always right

The idea behind this famous trading slogan may have been suggested by the hotelier César Ritz (1850–1918), who said in

SELFRIDGE'S London's New & Wonderful Shopping Centre ■ ■ ■
Dedicated to Woman's Service - devoted to the Children's Needs - the Man's Best Buying Place-with best assorted Stocks at London's Lowest Prices:
NOW OPEN TO THE WORLD   OXFORD STREET LONDON·W

"London receiving her Newest Institution"

1908, 'Le client n'a jamais tort' ('The customer is never wrong'). The American, Gordon Selfridge (1856–1947) is credited as the author of this ubiquitous statement. He came from Chicago and brought the concept of the large department store to Britain, and his shop opened in Oxford Street in 1909, adopting such slogans as 'This famous store needs no name on the door' and 'Complete satisfaction or money cheerfully refunded'. Gordon Selfridge is also credited as inventing the concept of so many 'shopping days until Christmas'.

Cut the mustard, to

A zesty and confident phrase meaning to do something well and efficiently, to prove oneself beyond all expectations at completing a task or occupation. The expression probably derives from mustard as slang for the best, possibly because it is hot or spicy; a line from O Henry's *Cabbages and Kings* (1894) reads,

> I'm not headlined in the bills but I'm the mustard in the salad just the same.

To cut, in this phrase, might refer to the harvesting of the plant, but it also might be used as in the expressions to 'cut a dash', 'cut up rough' or 'cut capers'.

Dear-John letter

A 'you're dumped' note from a wife or girlfriend breaking the news that the relationship with the recipient is over. The expression originated during the Second World War and is thought to be American. The unfortunate objects of Dear-John letters were usually members of the armed forces overseas, whose female partners at home had made new liaisons, proving that absence sometimes did not make the heart grow fonder.

Dekko, to take a
To glance at, or to have a quick look at. This is one of the many phrases that were brought back from India by the British Army in the colonial days in the late nineteenth century. In Hindi *dekho* is the imperative form of the verb *dekhna*, meaning to look at.

Devil – Between the devil and the deep blue sea
Between two evils, in a dilemma with nowhere to turn, to be between two equal dangers. The expression may be of nautical origin, the devil being a seam in the hull of a ship that ran along the waterline. Equally it could have been inspired by the phrase 'to steer or sail between Scylla and Charybdis'. In Homer's *Odyssey* Scylla was a six-headed monster that lived in a cavern overlooking a narrow channel off the coast of Sicily, who seized sailors from every passing ship with each of her six mouths. On the opposite rock Charybdis lived under a huge fig tree from where he sucked in and regorged the sea, forming a treacherous whirlpool. Odysseus sailed between these two perils, losing his ship in the whirlpool and the crew to Scylla. Only he survived by clinging to the fig tree.

A commonly used modern phrase with a mythical ring is 'between a rock and a hard place'.

Devil – Talk of the devil
This proverb, thought to have appeared in the seventeenth century should read, 'Talk of the devil and he's sure to appear', and 'Speak of the devil and he comes in person.' It is superstitious, as with most references to the devil, referred to in the Christian and Jewish faiths as the supreme spirit of evil, tempter of mankind and enemy of God. It means that if you talk about someone, they are

likely to appear unexpectedly. Most people now shorten the phrase to 'Talk of the devil'. The phrase may have come from an old proverb, 'Talk of the Dule and he'll put out his horns'.

> Forthwith the devil did appear,
> For blame him, and he's always near.
>
> Matthew Prior (1664–1721), *Hans Carvel* (1701)

And a more modern and optimistic version is, 'Talk of an angel and you'll hear the fluttering of its wings'.

Diamond – A diamond is forever

In 1939 the South African company De Beers launched an advertising campaign to promote the tradition of diamond engagement rings, using this as a catch line. It was created by copywriter BJ Kidd from the NW Ayer agency in Chicago, perhaps inspired by a line in Anita Loos's novel *Gentlemen Prefer Blondes* (1925; filmed in 1953): 'Kissing your hand may make you feel very, very good, but a diamond and sapphire bracelet lasts forever.' Ian Fleming put a new twist on the phrase in the title of his 1956 James Bond novel, *Diamonds are Forever*. The theme tune of the film, memorably sung by Shirley Bassey, has helped to perpetuate the phrase.

In fact diamonds are not forever, as they consist of pure carbon and will burn at extremely high temperatures.

Diamond – Diamond of the first water

An especially fine diamond, one of the greatest value for its size. The degree of brilliance or lustre of a diamond is called its water; and in the seventeenth century diamonds were classified as first water, second water and so on, the highest-quality gems being of the first water, that is, as pure as clear, limpid stream water. This method of grading died out before 1850, but the phrase remained in common usage. Hence 'of the first water' denotes the finest, or an extreme of some kind surpassing all others, whether good or bad; for instance, an 'artist of the first water' or a 'thief of the first water' or a 'gaffe of the first water'.

Did she fall or was she pushed?
Originally this phrase was used to ask, flippantly, how a young girl had lost her virginity. In 1908 the phrase was used in a different context in the news about the mysterious death of a certain Violet Charlesworth, whose body was found on the beach at the base of the cliffs at Beachy Head, and Thorne Smith wrote a comic novel *Did She Fall* in 1936. It is now used by headline writers about women who lose their jobs in dramatic circumstances.

Dig for victory
Food shortages in the early days of the Second World War in 1939 prompted the Ministry of Agriculture to encourage people to 'grow their own'. Only a month after the outbreak of war, on 4 October the Minister, Sir Reginald Dorman-Smith, said in a radio broadcast:

> Let's get going. Let 'Dig for Victory' be the motto of everyone with a garden and of every able-bodied man and woman capable of digging an allotment in their spare time.

Within two years the number of allotments in Britain had doubled, and 'rearing your own' became popular – especially pig keeping, with nearly 7,000 Pig Clubs in existence by the end of the war.

DINKY (Double Income, No Kids)
This phrase of the 1980s, better known by its acronym DINKY, refers to a couple with well-paid jobs and no offspring to support. It was one of a variety of new terms created in New York during the high-spending, high-earning early years of the 1980s. As with most Americanisms, these newly invented words travelled to Britain to describe various social sub-groups and relationships. YUPPIE means 'young upwardly (or urban) mobile professional person', then the craze really caught on and in 1986 NIMBY was born, which means 'not in my back yard', referring to folk who did not want building

development to take place which might spoil their view or their way of life. Today we have YETTIES, to describe those computer nerds who are 'young, entrepreneurial, technology-based'.

Divine Right of Kings, the

This is the hypothesis that kings reign by decree of God, notwithstanding the will of the people. This phrase was much used in the seventeenth century on account of the posturings of the Stuart kings. The idea that monarchs were answerable to God alone arose from the example of patriarchal rule set in the Old Testament. Monarchy based on primogeniture was held to be divinely anointed, and unquestioning obedience could therefore be demanded from the people. The theory was expounded in full by James I (1566–1635) in his True Law of Free Monarchies (1598) and Sir Robert Filmer's Patriarcha (1642, published 1680). Divine Right was suspended in Britain by Oliver Cromwell and his son Richard between 1649 and 1660. The phrase, however, remained in circulation and appears later from an early feminist voice.

> The divine right of husbands, like the divine right of kings, may, it is hoped, in this enlightened age, be contested without danger.
> Mary Wollstonecraft (1759–97),
> A Vindication of the Rights of Woman (1792)

Dog – A dog in a manger

A mean-spirited person who will not use something he has that is wanted by another, while not allowing the other to use it, or more

simply, someone who prevents another enjoying himself. The allusion is to Aesop's fable written in about 600 BC, of a dog that made his bed in a manger of hay. When an ox disturbed him he snarled and drove the ox away. He would not allow the ox to come near to eat the hay, but would not eat it himself. This story also suggests the wise advice of the old German expression 'Let sleeping dogs lie'.

Dog – A dog is for life not just for Christmas

An advertising slogan from the National Canine Defence League, probably from the 1980s, to promote the protection from cruelty of dogs given as Christmas gifts. This resilient phrase can be reworked in many convoluted ways such as 'A turkey is not just for Christmas, it's for Boxing Day, the day after, and the day after . . .', and from the *Independent* (1 February 1997), 'A Scottish parliament is not just for Christmas, it's for life'.

Dog – Every dog has its day

This is a commonly used phrase that seems to have appeared first in English in the writings of R Taverner in 1539 and subsequently in those of Shakespeare:

> Let Hercules himself do what he may,
> The cat will mew, and dog will have his day.

> *Hamlet* (1600)

It means that one may be enjoying good luck or success right now, but remember there's always a queue, so make way for the next person (see **Flavour of the month**, q.v.). This sentiment has been expressed for thousands of years. Rupert Brooke (1887–1915) gives the dog and his day a sentimental word in his poem, 'The Little Dog's Day'. The Latin proverb reads *Hodie mihi – cras tibi*, 'Today to me, tomorrow to thee'. And another ancient old wives' tale states that 'Fortune visits every man once, she favours me now, but she will favour you in your turn'.

Thus every dog at last will have his day –
He who this morning smiled, at night may sorrow,
The grub today's a butterfly tomorrow.

Peter Pindar (1738–1819), Odes to Condolence

Dog – The black dog has walked all over him

The metaphorical 'black dog' has various personalities. To be walked over or to be cursed by the 'black dog' means to be suffering from mental depression. Horace wrote that to see a black dog with its pups was a bad omen, and the devil has been frequently symbolized by a black dog. However, the phrase 'black dog' is eighteenth-century slang for a counterfeit silver coin made of washed pewter. Even then 'black' when applied to ill-begotten money was a familiar term. There is another phrase, 'to blush like a black dog', which means not to blush at all.

Dog – The dog days of summer

Very hot and oppressive summer days. The Romans called the hottest weeks of the summer *caniculares dies*, not because dogs are thought to go mad in the heat, although Noël Coward did write in 1932, that 'Mad dogs and Englishmen go out in the midday sun'. The theory was that the Dog Star, Sirius, the brightest star in the firmament, rises with the sun. It is an ancient belief that the combined heat of Sirius and the sun produced the stifling weather of the dog days, from about 3 July to 11 August. The film *Dog Day Afternoon* (1975) by Sidney Lumet, starring Al Pacino, is set on a day during these weeks and tells a story of two incompetent bank robbers, a tragi-comic tale based on a true newspaper story.

Dog – The hair of the dog that bit you

This phrase refers to a remedy usually administered to someone with a hangover, after an overindulgence of alcohol the night before. The theory is that the very thing that causes the malady is the best cure or means of relief, so another drink in the morning is considered by some the best pick-me-up, or by others a recipe to make one feel worse, not better. The general principle that 'like cures like' comes from Roman times, expressed in Latin as *similia similibus curantura*. The peculiar 'hair of the dog' phrase perhaps originated in the sixteenth century when if one was bitten by a mad dog, probably suffering from rabies, it was accepted medical practice to dress the wound with the burnt hair of the dog, as an antidote. Amazingly this cure was recommended for dog bites for about two hundred years until its efficacy was brought into question.

Dog – To see a man about a dog
This is a very shifty turn of phrase and suggests a cover-up. It is the excuse offered if one wishes to be discreet and avoid giving the true reason for leaving the room, the meeting or whatever social gathering. The phrase is often used as a euphemism for some unmentionable activity such as going to the lavatory or, worse, going to do something or meet someone one shouldn't. The phrase refers to betting on dog racing.

Do-it-yourself
A phrase that took hold after the Second World War during the boom in house ownership and the natural desire to carry out repairs and improvements cheaply. The phrase, commonly known by the mnemonic DIY, is the hobby if not obsession of the amateur builder, plumber or electrician. Nowadays householders are inspired by the 'do-it-yourself' television programmes such as the BBC's phenomenally popular *Changing Rooms*. The phrase is also used more widely to describe many other forms of self-help – including, jokingly, 'DIY brain surgery'.

Dragon's teeth, to sow
To stir up trouble, strife or war, to foster disagreement, or perhaps to act with the intention of putting an end to conflict, but to succeed only in starting it. The Philistines are supposed to have sown dragon's teeth when they captured Samson, bound him and

put out his eyes. Ethelred II did the same in 1002 when he ordered the massacre of the Danes on St Brice's Day, which started such fierce reprisals that he was eventually forced to flee, as did the Germans when they took Alsace-Lorraine from France in 1871. The reference is to the Greek myth of Cadmus. Cadmus was supposed to have introduced the alphabet to Greece and according to legend he killed the dragon that guarded the fountain of Dirce, in Boeotia, and sowed its teeth. From these sprang up a horde of warriors intent on killing him. On Athene's advice Cadmus threw a precious stone among them. The warriors set upon each other in the struggle to retrieve the stone until only five remained alive, and with Cadmus they founded Thebes. The teeth which Cadmus did not sow came into the hands of Aetes, King of Colchis, and one of the tasks he gave the hero Jason was to sow them and slay the armed warriors that rose from them.

Drunk as a lord, as
This simile must have first been observed in the eighteenth century when the consumption of alcohol was something well-bred gentlemen liked to boast about. There was a certain amount of pride in the amount of wine or port that could be consumed in one session. Indeed, gin was safer to drink than water at the time, and gout was a common affliction among the gentry.

Dust, to bite the dust
To fall down dead, alluding to falling off a horse. This expression derives from Wild West stories of violence and desperadoes, from the unstable western frontier in nineteenth-century America, before orderly settlements were established. It was in common use during the Second World

War, especially in the RAF. The phrase is now often heard as a chant to the tune of the song by Queen of the same name, in the form 'Another one bites the dust', when one contestant beats another – especially by the live audience for the television contest *Gladiators*.

Easy as pie, as

Making a pie is not easy and this expression must apply to the eating of it. An easy task can also be described as a 'piece of cake' which is also easy to obtain and eat, as opposed to baking it. It could also refer to the Greek letter pi or P, which stands for the number 3.14 and forms part of a number of mathematical formulas – though not 'easy', pi does simplify the calculations.

Elephant and Castle

This is not only a district in south-east London, but also the sign of a public house at Newington Butts, the name of an Underground station and a pink shopping centre on a very busy roundabout in that area. A common sight in ancient times were the war elephants that were used to transport archers and armed knights who travelled in 'castles' (howdahs) mounted on the animals' backs. Another popular derivation is that the name is a corruption of the disparaging name, 'Infanta de Castile', referring to Eleanor of Castile, young wife of Edward I (1239–1307), who, incidentally, was known as 'Longshanks' because of his tall stature. The Elephant and Castle motif is used as the crest of the Cutlers Company, which traded extensively in ivory.

England expects every man to do his duty

Admiral Lord Nelson's famous signal to his fleet before the Battle of Trafalgar in 1805. The intended signal was 'England confides every man to do his duty', but much to the signalman's consternation, the word 'confide' was not included in the signal book, so he sought permission to substitute the word 'expects', which meant that he did not have to hoist seven flags, one for each letter of the word 'confide'. The original meaning of the word 'confide' is to entrust knowledge of one's private affairs, so Lord Nelson meant to put his trust in his men to do their duty in his plan of battle. The sentiment of this slogan was later revived in many a Victorian bedroom, in a call to reluctant or shy wives, to be brave, do their patriotic duty and 'lie back and think of England'.

English disease, the
The poor old English have been blamed for many complaints and *malaises* over the years. Since Columbus's time the French have described syphilis as the English disease, and the English retort to this insult was to call it the French disease. The French term for the onset of menstruation is *les Anglais sont arrivés*. Later, after the Industrial Revolution the damp English climate combined with sooty smog meant that bronchitis was prevalent, and it became known as the English disease all over the world. Now some social ailments tend to be described as English, including class differences, poor industrial relations and economic stagnation. In the 1950s and 1960s under the all-powerful trade unions, industrial strikes were widely known as the English disease. More recently, football hooliganism, both at home and abroad, has been dubbed the English disease.

Every cloud has a silver lining
In every situation, no matter how seemingly hopeless and gloomy, there is always some redeeming brightness to be found if one takes the trouble to look for it – while there's life there's hope. This

optimistic guidance to look on the bright side has been around since Roman times (although one Latin proverb reads, 'After the sun, the clouds'). In a similar sixteenth-century proverb it all depends whose side you are on: 'The death of wolves is the safety of sheep' (see **Wind**, q.v.) – good news for sheep, bad news for wolves. In Milton's *Comus* (1634), the lady lost in the wood resolves not to give up hope, and says,

> Was I deceived or did a sable cloud
> Turn forth her silver lining on the night?
> I did not err: there does a sable cloud
> Turn forth her silver lining on the night.

And, not forgetting the cynic, Noël Coward included these lines in his 1952 song, 'There Are Bad Times Just Around the Corner':

> There are dark clouds hurtling through the sky,
> And it's no good whining
> About a silver lining,
> For we know from experience that they won't roll by.

Every picture tells a story
This is thought to be a modern proverb, although Charlotte Brontë alludes to it in *Jane Eyre* (1847):

> The letter press . . . I cared little for . . . Each picture told a story.

In 1904 the phrase was used with a picture of a man bent over, clutching his back in pain to advertise Doan's Backache Kidney Pills. The pop singer Rod Stewart released an album with this title in the 1970s. The catchphrase has been adapted for many other situations, and in a development of the idea the well-used phrase 'One picture is worth a thousand words' rings true for some, although others might say, 'Pictures are the books of the unlearned' (1662; found in *Tilley's Dictionary of Proverbs*, 1950).

Everything in the garden is lovely
A colloquial phrase to say, all's well, there's not a worry in the world. The expression comes from George Le Brunn and JP

Harrington's song 'Everything in the garden's lovely' of 1898, made popular by Marie Lloyd (1870–1922). Gardens have symbolized paradise since biblical times and the Garden of Eden in which Adam was placed by God (Genesis 2:15). The name is Hebrew in origin and means 'place of pleasure', and the Garden of Eden was traditionally said to be situated in Mesopotamia. Fertile land tends to be referred to as a garden, such as Kent, the Garden of England; Italy is known as the Garden of Europe and Sicily is the Garden of Italy. In the 1920s the highly suggestive song 'Come Into the Garden, Maud' (a setting of Tennyson's poem of 1855) had something entirely different in mind. The phrase is still used today, and in these more cynical times, with an ironic tone, to indicate that perhaps everything in the garden is not quite as lovely as it could be.

Exception that proves the rule, the

This strange phrase has been in use since the seventeenth century. It seems to mean the very opposite of what it is actually trying to say, and it is often misused to mean that a particular exception proves the correctness of a rule, rather than putting it to the test. However, the word 'prove' here is used in its meaning to 'test'. So the phrase makes more sense, that an exception tests the truth of a rule. Alternatively perhaps 'prove' is used in the context of baking, as dough is left to 'prove' or rise before it is baked, and it might be meant that the exception must 'rise' to meet the demands of the rule in question. Because of the general confusion over the years, this proverb has embraced the additional meaning 'no rule is so general that it cannot embrace some exception'.

Eye for an eye, a tooth for a tooth, an

Punishment equal to the crime, retaliation in kind or simply getting even. The justification for this form of retribution comes from the Old Testament.

Eye for eye, tooth for tooth, hand for hand, foot for foot.

Exodus 21:24

Jesus referred to these words in the New Testament and put his own spin on their message, creating another commonly used expression, 'to turn the other cheek':

> Ye have heard that it hath been said, An eye for an eye, and a tooth for a tooth: But I say unto you, That ye resist not evil: but whosoever shall smite thee on thy right cheek, turn to him the other also.

Matthew 5:39–9

Face that launched a thousand ships, the

The face is that of the legendary beauty, Helen of Troy, and the ships were the Greek fleet, which sailed for Troy to avenge the King of Sparta. In Greek legend Helen was the daughter of Zeus and Leda, and wife of Menelaus, King of Sparta. She eloped with Paris, Prince of Troy, and the angry Menelaus sent a thousand ships to lay siege to the city of Troy. The fabled Helen is now an archetype of female beauty.

The phrase itself was first written by Christopher Marlowe (1564–93):

> Was this the face that launched a thousand ships,
> And burned the topless towers of Ilium?

Doctor Faustus (1604)

The story of Helen of Troy is father to other words of wisdom such as 'Beware Greeks bearing gifts', or 'I fear Greeks even when they offer gifts' (Virgil, *Aeneid*, 1 BC). After the ten-year siege of the city of Troy heroes had been slain on both sides, Achilles the Brave and Ajax the Proud lay dead, and the Trojan Paris was dead too. Only Helen remained as lovely as ever, a precious prize locked in Troy. One of the Greek survivors, Odysseus, devised an ingenious plan to invade the city by hiding all his men in a wooden horse, which the Trojans mistakenly took to be a tribute from their beaten enemy. Finally the victorious Greeks escorted Helen, ever since known as Helen of Troy, back to Greece and the house of King Menelaus.

Famous for fifteen minutes, to be

Meaning to have short-lived fame, of the type that is now quite possible in the modern, media-obsessed age. This expression comes from the celebrated words in a catalogue for an exhibition of Andy Warhol's work in Stockholm in 1968. Pop artist Warhol (1928–87) was concerned, amongst other subjects, with the nature of celebrity and he wrote, 'In the future everyone will be world famous for fifteen minutes.' Andy Warhol was described by Gore Vidal as the only genius he knew with an IQ of 60. The phrase struck a chord and can now be shortened to, 'He's had his fifteen minutes'. *Famous for Fifteen Minutes* was the title of a series of 'Where are they now?' programmes lasting fifteen minutes on BBC Radio 4 from 1990, which featured faded 'movers and shakers' who were recalled from obscurity to account for their decline.

Fast lane, to live life in the

This is a metaphor meaning to live dangerously, indulgently and expensively, and dates from the late 1970s, probably coined by newspaper headline writers. The fast lane is the outer lane of a motorway where traffic overtakes or travels at high speed. It is naturally associated with fast cars, and in an advertisement for Toshiba computers in 1989 the strapline read, 'Jackie Stewart lives life in the fast lane – like any businessman really'. The opposite metaphor, of course, is to be stranded on the hard shoulder of life.

Feather in one's cap, a

A personal achievement or honour to be proud of. The feather is a proud and visible emblem of victory and the gesture of putting a feather in your hat is almost universal in one form or another. The allusion is to the ancient custom, widespread in Asia, among American Indians and throughout Europe of adding a feather to the headgear to mark each enemy killed. Indeed, today's sportsman who kills his first woodcock puts a feather from the bird in his hat. At one time in Hungary the only person who could wear a feather was someone who had killed a Turk. When General Charles Gordon (1833–85), known as Chinese Gordon, quelled the Taiping rebellion in 1864 he was honoured by the Chinese government with the 'yellow jacket and peacock's feather'.

Field day, to have a field day

A figurative expression for a day or occasion or time of particular excitement, often a day away from the usual routine. The phrase is in fact a military term for a day when troops have manoeuvres, exercises or reviews – out in the field. (The military refer to the area or sphere of operations as 'the field'.) In the  American Navy it is a day devoted to cleaning ship in preparation for inspection. School children enjoy field trips on which they travel away from school, particularly to study geography.

Fine fettle, in

To be in good order or condition – 'fettle' is an old word meaning condition, order or shape. Nowadays, it rarely appears on its own, being usually heard in the alliterative phrase. In the past we might have heard 'good fettle' or 'bad fettle', and in *John Barleycorn* by Jack London, published in 1913:

> Those fifty-one days of fine sailing and intense sobriety had put me in splendid fettle.

The origin of the word fettle is somewhat obscure. It probably comes from the Old English *fetel* for a belt, so fettle first meant to gird oneself up, as for a heavy task. It is related to the German *Fessel* for a chain or band, but not to the similar 'fetter', which actually comes from the same root as 'foot'. In English the word was most typically used as a verb meaning to put things in order, tidy up, arrange, or prepare. In Anne Brontë's *Agnes Grey* (1847), in the Yorkshire dialect speech of a servant:

But next day, afore I'd gotten fettled up – for indeed, Miss, I'd no heart to sweeping an' fettling, an' washing pots; so I sat me down i' th' muck – who should come in but Maister Weston.

In northern English dialects it is sometimes used in the sense of making or repairing something. In Australia, a 'fettler' is a railway maintenance worker. It is also used in some manufacturing trades – in metal casting and pottery it describes the process of knocking the rough edges off a piece.

Fingerlickin' good, It's
An enduring advertising slogan for Kentucky Fried Chicken, first used by the company in 1952. Many songs used the expression in the 1960s and 1970s, and Lonnie Smith had a hit with his album, *Fingerlickin' Good Soul Organ* in 1968. The description 'finger-licking' is probably jargon used by Southern American black jazz musicians, most likely guitarists; however, the *OED* records the phrase as early as 1860.

Flavour of the month
A generic American advertising phrase of the mid-1940s attempting to persuade shoppers to buy a new flavour of ice cream each month and not just stick to their usual choice. Since then it has been used to describe any short-lived fashion, craze or person, popularly referred to as being 'flavoursome', and then quickly dropped after a period of being in demand.
The metaphorical possibilities of the word 'ambush' are currently catching on in several areas of activity in the USA, making it the lexical flavour of the month in American English.

Flynn – To be in like Flynn
A ribald phrase that means to take instant advantage of any chance that might be up for grabs. More particularly it means not to miss an opportunity of seducing a woman. Flynn of the phrase is ' the Tasmanian-born film star, Errol Flynn (1909–59), who led one

of Hollywood's most adventurous lives, both on and off screen. His swashbuckling lifestyle enthralled millions of fans for twenty years, but it got the better of him by the end of his life. The phrase was widely used in the Second World War. It is said that Flynn himself was not flattered by it, despite his own tendency to boast about his sexual conquests.

Foot – To put one's foot in it

To make an inadvertent blunder, particularly to say the wrong thing and get yourself into 'deep doo-doo'. To make a *faux pas*, which literally means a false step. From the Irish 'bull', 'Every time I open my mouth I put my foot in it'. Bull is an old fashioned word for a verbal blunder, and the Irish seem to have been associated with this trait. Bull may have been named after the Irish Lawyer, Obadiah Bull, who worked in London in the fifteenth century and was notorious for his mistakes. Another explanation is that it comes from the contradiction in Papal Bulls in which the Pope humbly styles himself 'servant of servants', while asserting complete authority. Since the 1970s the habit of making verbal *faux pas* has been called 'foot-in-mouth disease' following a serious outbreak of foot-and-mouth disease, a contagious viral disease of cattle, sheep, goats and pigs. Prince Philip, with something of a reputation for saying the wrong thing at the wrong time, calls the affliction, 'dentopedalogy'.

Forty winks, to take

A colloquial term for a short nap or a doze. Quite why shutting one eye forty times has come to mean a quick snooze is unclear, but it could have something to do with the fact that the number forty appears frequently in the scriptures and used to be thought of as a holy number. Moses was on the Mount for forty days and forty nights, Elijah was fed by ravens for forty days, the rain of the Flood fell forty days and another forty days passed before Noah opened the window of the ark. Christ fasted for forty days and he was seen forty days after his Resurrection. Modern colloquialisms for a quick nap include a 'zizz', 'to catch a few zeds' alluding to the zeds drawn in cartoons indicating that the character is asleep, the zeds replicating the sound of their breathing. Busy people and politicians who work late into the night maintain their faculties by taking 'a power nap'.

Fourth dimension, the

The three known dimensions are length, breadth and height. The fourth dimension, or space–time continuum, is defined as reality. In the fourth dimension the infinite number of solids in the universe react with each other through time and energy. As a mathematical concept a hypothetical fourth dimension is related to the recognized three dimensions and exists in parallel with their relation with each other. In 1921 Albert Einstein (1879–1955) introduced time as the fourth dimension in his Theory of Relativity. And here we get very New Age; in the time domain, the fourth dimension continues the movement of the third dimension (the past) to form a wave, constituting fractally the space-time continuum. Not surprisingly, the expression is sometimes used to describe that which is beyond the limits of normal experience.

French leave, to take

This is leave of absence without permission or without announcing one's departure, particularly referring to soldiers taking unauthorized leave. Rivalry between the British and the French has lasted for hundreds of years and this phrase alludes to the eighteenth-century French custom of leaving without saying goodbye to one's host, if one had a pressing engagement, in order not to disrupt the party, or to disconcert the host. This was naturally interpreted by the British as extremely bad manners. Not to be outdone, the French later associated the habit with the English, however. Hence their equivalent for French leave is *s'en aller à l'anglaise*. An earlier

French insult was the sixteenth-century slang for a creditor, which was *un Anglais*. Even Shakespeare got in on the act:

> France is a dog hole.
>
> *All's Well That Ends Well*

Friend – A friend in need is a friend indeed
This is a Latin proverb from the sayings of Ennius (239–169 BC) and reads *Amicus certus in re incerta cernitur* – 'a sure friend is made known when (one is) in difficulty'. Whatever the truth of this wise old saying there have been numerous plays on its words over the centuries as it often transpires that 'a friend in need, is a pest indeed'. Or according to Kin Hubbard, 'A friend that ain't in need is a friend indeed'. And this witticism was seen on an old postcard: 'A friend in need is a friend indeed, but who needs a friend in need?'

Frying pan – To jump out of the frying pan into the fire
To leap from one bad predicament to another which is as bad or even worse. In short, to go from bad to worse. Most languages have an equivalent phrase, and the French have *tomber de la poêle dans le feu/la braise*, from which the English is probably translated. The Greeks have, 'out of the smoke into the flame'; the Italians and Portuguese, 'to fall from the frying pan into the coals'; and the Gaelic is, 'out of the cauldron into the fire'. The phrase can be traced back to about 1530 when, in the course of a religious argument, Sir Thomas More, Henry VIII's Lord Chancellor and author of *Utopia*, accused William Tyndale, translator of the Bible into English, that he 'featly conuayed himself out of the frying panne fayre into the fyre'. Unfortunately both men met a gruesome end. Sir Thomas More was hanged as a traitor in 1535 for not approving of the marriage between Henry VIII and Anne Boleyn, and Tyndale was publicly strangled and burned as a heretic in 1536.

Full Monty, the
Everything, the lot, the complete works. Said of anything done to the utmost or fullest degree. The origin of the expression is uncertain. It may derive from the 'full amount', or the Spanish card game *monte* (literally mountain or heap of cards), or it may refer to the full three-piece Sunday Best suit from the men's outfitters Montagu Burton. The full English breakfast – bacon, eggs, sausage, black pudding, beans, fried bread – that is, the works – was popularly known as the 'Full Monty' after the Second World War because Field Marshal Sir Bernard Montgomery, nicknamed 'Monty' (1887–1976), was said to have started every day with a full English breakfast when campaigning in North Africa. The British phrase became familiar generally in the English-speaking world from the 1997 film *The Full Monty*, directed by Peter Cattaneo, about a group of unemployed factory workers from Sheffield who raise money by staging a strip act at a local club.

Full tilt, at full tilt
At full speed or full force. The expression probably originated in the fourteenth century when 'tilting at the quintain' was a popular sport among medieval knights. A dummy head, often representing a Turk or Saracen, was fastened to rotate around an upright stake fixed in the ground. At full speed, the knight on horseback tilted towards the head with his lance and if he failed to strike it in the

right place it would spin round and strike him in the back before he could get clear. Londoners used to tilt from boats, the quintain being fixed to a mast erected in the Thames. Tilting at the quintain remained a rustic sport especially popular at wedding celebrations until the mid-seventeenth century. The similar phrase 'to tilt at windmills' has a rather different meaning, namely, to stand up to fanciful enemies. The reference is to the crazed knight Don Quixote (in Cervantes's novel, *Don Quixote*, 1605) who imagined the windmills to be giants and advanced to attack. The gentle, if mad, knight with his dreams of chivalry has given his name to the English language in the adjective 'quixotic', used to describe a romantic idealist with wildly unrealistic ideas of honour and doing good.

Game as Ned Kelly, as

To possess fighting spirit or energy for some dynamic activity, or in modern parlance, 'up for it'. The phrase refers to the infamous Australian desperado, bushranger and folk hero Ned Kelly (1855–80), who after legendary exploits including robbery and murder, was captured with his brother Dan wearing roughly made suits of armour, after a battle with the police, and hanged at Melbourne. True to form, his last words were 'Such is life'.

Garbage in garbage out

A term from typesetting and computing known by 1964 and sometimes abbreviated to GIGO, meaning that if you put incorrect data into a computer, however much you embellish it, what comes out will be meaningless and useless. In the wider sense it conveys the simple idea that you get back what you put in, reflected in the sixteenth-century proverb, 'There comes nothing out of a sack but what was in it.' It could never be argued that this phrase came from Roman times, but there is a charming Latin translation, *Purgamentum init, exit purgamentum*.

Genghis Khan – Somewhere to the right of Genghis Khan
This cliché describes someone whose views are extremely right wing. Genghis Khan (1162–1227) was the founder of the Moghul Empire. His original name was Temujin and he was given the title 'Genghis Khan', which literally means 'King of the Ocean'. He acquired a fighting force of some 20,000 tribesmen and through sheer brutality and relentless raping and pillaging, overcame the Mongolian and Tartar peoples, and by 1206 he was acknowledged overlord of Mongolia. Eventually his empire extended from China to the Adriatic Sea and his son reached the walls of Budapest.

Arthur Scargill, president of the National Union of Mineworkers said in 1982, 'Of course, in those days, the union leaders were well to the right of Genghis Khan.'

Giddy goat, to act the
To fool around. Goats are noted for their unpredictable behaviour. In the literal sense giddy means insane or to be 'possessed by a god'. In Latin goat is *caper* and goats are noted for their frivolous and frisky nature. To cut a caper means to skip or leap about playfully.

Go – To boldly go where no man has gone before
A claim made in part of the title sequence to the popular TV space adventure series, *Star Trek* (see **Beam me up Scotty**, q.v.). The mission of the Starship *Enterprise* to explore outer space still attracts millions of regular viewers all over the world. The expressed aim 'to boldly go' became possibly the most celebrated split infinitive of the twentieth century. Its wide use, often in parody, has meant that we all know how to break this particular rule of English grammar.

Go for it!
A very popular encouragement in wide use during the 1980s. It may come from the keep-fit exercise of aerobics, which was all the

rage at the time. In Jane Fonda's book (1981) and video (1983) she exhorted, 'Go for the burn, go for it!' The burn is the sensation felt in the muscles during the workout. President Reagan said, 'America, go for it', in 1985, of tax reform. Victor Kiam, American razor entrepreneur, entitled his 1986 memoirs, *Going For It*. British Airways coined, 'Go for it, America' to persuade Americans to ignore current terrorist threats and visit Europe. Media mogul and, coincidentally, Jane Fonda's husband, Ted Turner, was called a 'Go-for-it guy'. 'To go for it' was also a vulgar Australian term from the mid-1920s meaning 'extremely eager for sexual intercourse'.

Go to work on an egg

The British Egg Marketing Board launched a high-profile advertising campaign in 1957 with this catch-line. Fay Weldon (1932–), later well known as a novelist and television playwright, was at the time a copywriter at the Mather & Crowther agency. She is modest about the authorship of the line, saying, 'It is perfectly possible that I put those particular six words together in that particular order, but I would not swear to it.'

Goal posts, to move the

A colloquial expression derived from football meaning to change the agreed conditions or rules for carrying out a plan, quite often in business when clients change their minds after work on a project has already begun. The implication is that 'to move the goal posts' involves some attempt to gain unfair advantage over an opponent, or generally to upset him.

Seen in the *Guardian*, 1 March 1989, about the imposition of a new railway line in Kent:

The people of Kent vote solidly for the Conservative Party . . . Why are these people, therefore, trying to move the goalposts after the football match has started?

Gone for a Burton

Absent, missing or lost, dead or presumed dead. The expression was common among service personnel in the Second World War. There are several theories as to its origin. One possibility is that it refers to the training of RAF wireless operators in a Blackpool Burton's clothing store. Those who failed their test were said to have 'gone for a Burton' and it was subsequently applied to those who were killed. Another popular theory is that the town of Burton is famous for its beer, and that to have 'Gone for a Burton' is a euphemism to explain someone's absence because they have gone for a beer. Extending this usage, the sea is known as 'the drink', so when sailors or airmen were killed at or over the sea, other servicemen referred to them, with a certain amount of black humour, as 'gone for a Burton'.

Gone with the wind

A wistful saying to describe events that have occurred, but have left no trace. The phrase comes from Ernest Dowson's poem 'Non Sum Qualis Eram', also known as 'Cynara' (1896):

> I have forgot much, Cynara! Gone with the wind,
> Flung roses, roses, riotously, with the throng.

It is the title of one of America's most widely read novels, written by Margaret Mitchell, published in 1936, and filmed by David O Selznick in 1939. The phrase refers to the Southern United States before the American Civil War (1861–5). The on-screen prologue of the film reads:

> There was a land of Cavaliers and Cotton Fields called the Old South. Here in this patrician world the Age of Chivalry took its last bows. Here was the last ever seen of the Knights and their Ladies fair, of Master and Slave. Look for it only in books, for its is no more than a dream remembered, a Civilization gone with the wind . . .

The story concerns an egotistical Southern girl, played by

Vivien Leigh, who survives the Civil War, but loses the only man she cares for.

Gordon Bennett

A mild oath, similar to, 'Oh God'. In fact, 'Gawd' and St Bennett (or Benet) have been put forward as the pair behind this expletive; St Benet is short for St Benedict. Shakespeare has in *Twelfth Night* (1600) 'the bells of St Bennet' possibly from the church, St Bennet Hithe, Paul's Wharf, opposite the Globe theatre. However, it seems more likely that the said Gordon Bennett was James Gordon Bennett (1841–1918), the editor-in-chief of the *New York Herald*, who was responsible for sending Henry Morton Stanley to find Dr David Livingstone in Africa. Extravagant and extrovert, he gave his name to a motor race held in France in the 1900s where he resided after a scandal in America. Such was his profile in society that there is a street in Paris named Avenue Gordon-Bennett. In English the similarity between Gordon and Gawd must have struck a chord and this expletive, which is still used today, was born. At the turn of the nineteenth century people shied away from blasphemy in the name of God, so 'Gorblimey' evolved instead of 'God blind me', and WC Fields used to cry out, 'Godfrey Daniel!' in place of 'God damn you!', but the identity of Godfrey Daniel can only be guessed at.

Great balls of fire!

A famous hit song for Jerry Lee Lewis in 1957 written by Jack Hammer and Otis Blackwell. It was first heard in public as a cry of surprise in the 1939 film **Gone With the Wind** (q.v.)and is presumably derived from the Deep South of America.

Green-eyed monster, the

To be jealous of or covet someone's beauty, achievements, attainment or wealth. The simile is commonly known as to be 'green with envy'. The monster was identified by Shakespeare in *Othello* (1602–4):

> IAGO: O! beware, my lord, of jealousy;
> It is the green ey'd monster which doth mock
> The meat it feeds on.

A greenish complexion was formerly held to be indicative of jealousy, not queasiness which is more likely, and it has been observed that all cats with green eyes 'mock the meat they feed on', so jealousy taunts its victim by both loving and hating it. However, to accuse someone of having 'green in their eye' is to suggest that they are inexperienced or easily bamboozled, as in 'greenhorn', which means to be a novice, green behind the ears, like the green horns of a young horned animal.

And Shakespeare again, in *Antony and Cleopatra* (1606–7):

My salad days,
When I was green in judgment . . .

Green wellie-brigade, the
A posse of Sloane Rangers, or those members of the upper classes who practise the country pursuits of hunting, shooting and fishing. Green Wellington boots as typically worn by country folk take their name from Arthur Wellesley, first Duke of Wellington (1769–1852). The term Sloane Rangers was coined by style commentator Peter York in *Harper's and Queen* in the 1970s, in a pun combining Sloane Street or Sloane Square, London habitats of these types, with 'Lone Ranger', from the popular television cowboy series of the 1960s. Sloane Rangers were also commonly known as 'Headscarf Harriets', and their men as 'Hooray Henrys', shortened to 'Hoorays'.

Half cock, to go off at
To be unsuccessful at doing something due to inadequate preparation, or being in too much of a hurry, reminiscent of the phrase 'more haste less speed', or simply 'be prepared'. This is probably an eighteenth-century expression when a musket which was cocked half-way had the hammer set in the safety position, to prevent accidental discharge. However, the mechanisms were sometimes faulty and the gun would fire, much to the surprise of the musketeer. It is thought that the term is simply related to hunting and shooting, though modern guns cannot in fact 'go off'

when they are half cocked. However, a hunter, carried away in the thrill of the chase and sighting his quarry, may raise the gun and press the trigger while still at half cock, so the gun does not fire.

Hanged, drawn and quartered
The correct order for this form of torturous capital punishment was that the victim was 'drawn, hanged, drawn, beheaded and quartered'. The crime that merited this sort of punishment was high treason against crown and country. The guilty were to be drawn to the place of execution on a hurdle or dragged along by horse's tail. Drawn also meant to be disembowelled, and this was added to the punishment in between the hanging stage and the quartering stage. Thus the sentence passed on the Scottish patriot Sir William Wallace in August 1305 was that he should be drawn from the Palace of Westminster to the Tower of London, then hanged until nearly dead, disembowelled, then beheaded and finally quartered. His quarters were gibbeted at Newcastle, Berwick, Stirling and Perth.

Happiness is egg shaped
Still working on the egg account, Fay Weldon did write the phrase 'Happiness is egg shaped' (see **Go to work on an egg**, q.v.) although she was probably inspired by Charles M Schultz's title for a Peanuts cartoon book in 1962, *Happiness is a warm puppy* ('. . . with an empty bladder' was added by some wag). The advertising and greetings-card worlds were inspired and a host of strap-lines were born, most famously 'Happiness is a cigar called Hamlet' (1970). In typical style songwriters Lennon and McCartney emphasized the dark side when they wrote 'Happiness is a warm gun' (1970). For centuries man has tried to define the essence of this most elusive of sensations. Rousseau (1712–78) said:

Happiness is a good bank account, a good cook, a good digestion.

Samuel Johnson declared in 1766:

Happiness consists in the multiplicity of agreeable consciousness.

And more recently we see:

Happiness is just a state of mind . . . like insanity.

Happy – As happy as Larry

This is another expression that means to be extremely happy, but the question is, 'Who was Larry?' It is believed to be an Australian expression from the late nineteenth century, and Larry may have been the boxer Larry Foley (1847–1917). The word may also relate to 'larrikin', an Australian term for a young hoodlum given to acts of rowdiness. Larrikins were particularly active on the streets in the 1880s and wore distinctive neat and colourful clothing.

Happy – As happy as a sandboy

This means to be very happy or in high spirits. It is a traditional expression from the late nineteenth and early twentieth centuries, when sandboys or men drove their donkeys through the streets selling bags of sand taken from beaches. The sand was used by householders for their gardens, by builders, and by publicans for sanding their floors. The merriness  of the sandboys was probably due, in some part, to the temptation of spending their takings in the hostelries to which they delivered the sand.

Hash, to settle someone's

To subdue or silence someone in no uncertain terms, or to sort out a muddle for them. A hash in this case is a jumble, mess or hotch-potch, from the dish of stewed mixed meat, potatoes and other vegetables. To 'make a hash of' means to bungle or make a mess of something. The verb 'settle' is often used to denote an active or somewhat forceful method of resolving a situation. Strictly speaking, to 'settle a score' is to settle accounts, and the phrase can be used to mean to settle financial debts, but it is more likely to be said when taking revenge for an injury or getting even with someone.

Another culinary expression with much the same meaning is to 'cook someone's goose'.

Hat – At the drop of a hat

On signal, instantly, without delay. The expression alludes to the American frontier practice of dropping a hat as a signal for a boxing or wrestling match to begin, usually the only formality observed. Athletics or horse races used to be started by the fast downward sweep of a hat. The expression has come to mean that one will do something with very little encouragement, or without delay. Hence the title of a revue, *At the Drop of a Hat*, starring Michael Flanders and Donald Swann, whose follow-up was entitled *At the Drop of Another Hat* (1963).

There are many sayings including the word 'hat', such as 'hats off to him', 'as black as your hat', 'I'll eat my hat' and many more that probably originated in the days when dress codes and social etiquette were more formal, requiring people in polite society to cover their heads.

Hat – To throw one's hat into the ring

To enter a contest or to become a candidate for office. This expression relates to the old custom of throwing one's hat into the boxing ring as the sign of accepting the pugilist's challenge.

Hatches, matches and despatches

A long-established and charmingly poetic colloquialism for a newspaper's announcements of births, marriages and deaths.

Have a banana

Britain became aware of the joys of bananas in the early 1900s, thanks to the efforts of a certain Roger Ackerley of Elders & Fyffes, banana importers, in 1898. This rhythmic phrase was never an official advertising slogan, but, 'Have a banana', was popularly added to the end of the first line of the song 'Let's All Go Down the Strand' (1904). The composer had not written it in, but it was so successful that the line was later added to the lyrics. Sales of bananas rocketed. Other banana songs soon followed. With

undisguised innuendo the song 'Burlington Bertie from Bow' (1914) includes, 'I've had a banana with Lady Diana'. 'Yes, we have no bananas' was allegedly proclaimed by a Greek fruit seller, and in 1923 *Punch* described it as 'the latest catchword'. The suggestive nature of the banana was celebrated again in 1959 with the slogan, 'Unzip a banana'.

Heath Robinson, it's a bit Heath Robinson
A phrase applied to an absurdly complicated mechanical contraption, especially one performing a basically simple action – some fantastic and ingenious apparatus usually with moving parts joined by bits of string and held together with a lick and a promise. The name is that of the highly imaginative William Heath Robinson (1872–1944) whose amusing cartoons of daft inventions, which appeared in *Punch* and elsewhere, captured the public imagination. Heath Robinson's absurd gadgets were seen as a caricature of the age of the machine and the humour often came from the expressions of the solemn onlookers inspecting the machines.

Here's mud in your eye!
A drinking toast, the sentiments of which could be read either way. One interpretation is that it is to wish good fortune, originating in the trenches of the First World War when soldiers would naturally rather mud was thrown in their eye than anything more lethal. Another, somewhat less good-natured, theory comes from horse racing, in which, with one's own horse out in front, it will be kicking mud into the eyes of the slower runners behind.

High jump, for the high jump
English slang for being in big trouble, also known these days as 'deep doo-doo' or 'deep shit'. It usually implies that dismissal or serious punishment are on the cards. The allusion is to the hanging of a convicted criminal, the gallows being 'the high jump', which was the former British judicial method for capital punishment.

Hoist with one's own petard
To be beaten with one's own weapons, or to be caught in one's own trap. The modern equivalent relates to the sport of football, 'to

score an own goal'. Shakespeare puts the petard in context when he has Hamlet say:

> For 'tis the sport to have the engineer
> Hoist with his own petard.

Hamlet (1600)

In 1600 a petard was a newly invented iron device used for blowing up walls, barricades or gates with gunpowder. It was a metal bell-shaped grenade filled with five or six pounds of gunpowder, dug into a trench and set off by a fuse. The devices were often unreliable and went off unexpectedly, and the engineer who fired the petard might be blown up by the explosion. Hence the expression, in which 'hoist' means to be lifted up, is an understated description of being blown up by your own bomb. The name of the device came from the Latin *petare* meaning to break wind, and the phrase is perhaps an ironic comment on the noise of the explosion. The 1979 film *Le Pétomane* starred Leonard Rossiter (1926–84) as Joseph Pujol, the tuneful wind-breaker who gained something of a reputation all over Europe as a musical performer at the end of the nineteenth century.

Hold the mayo

This is one of many urban buzz phrases of the ubiquitous takeaway food and drinks culture of the 1990s. When ordering a sandwich to 'take out', or take away, the order 'hold the mayo' means to serve the burger or sandwich without mayonnaise. The American chain of coffee shops, Starbucks and the like, are spawning a whole new language with buzz phrases such as 'a tall decaff latte with wings', 'a large triple shot cappuccino to fly', or 'wake up and smell the coffee', which means 'get your brain in gear'.

Horse – Don't look a gift horse in the mouth

Do not question the value or something given to you; it is very bad form to inspect a gift for faults or defects, so be grateful for anything received and, as the old saying goes, 'it's the thought that counts'.

This is an old proverb that has probably been in use for hundreds of years. The phrase has been discovered in the writings of St Jerome, one of the Latin Fathers of the fourth century, who identified it as a common proverb. No doubt the phrase alludes to the method of assessing the age of a horse by inspecting the number and condition of its teeth. The proverb also occurs in French, German, Italian, Spanish and other European languages.

Horse – Straight from the horse's mouth
Some knowledge received direct from the highest authority, from the person whose word need not be doubted. The expression comes from horse racing and has to do with the age of the steeds. The only certain way of discovering the age of a horse is by examining its teeth, especially those of the lower jaw. The first permanent horse teeth appear in the centre of the jaw at the age of two and a half. A year later a second pair appears and at between four and five years, the third pair appears. So, no matter what an owner may say about a horse's age, the evidence is there, straight in the horse's mouth.

Hour – at the eleventh hour
Just in the nick of time, at the last moment, before the end of the day. The allusion is to Jesus's parable of the labourers hired to work in the vineyard in which those starting work at the eleventh hour, that is late in the afternoon at about 5 o'clock, were paid the same as those who had 'borne the burden and heat of the day' (Matthew 20:1–16). The armistice ending the First World War came into effect at the eleventh hour of the eleventh day of the eleventh month.

How to win friends and influence people
Self-improvement courses date back to the early 1900s, and this phrase summed up the principle of Dale Carnegie's (1888–1955)

courses aimed at business people in America. In 1936 the phrase caught on with a worldwide audience when it was the title of Carnegie's best-selling book about business psychology. Following Carnegie's lead, Sheperd Mead published a book entitled *How to Succeed in Business Without Really Trying* in 1953, which was made into a musical in 1961 and a film in 1967.

How's your father?

A purely rhetorical question that originated as a humorous catchphrase in the music halls before the First World War. It later came to be a synonym for 'nonsense' or meaningless ritual and it is a useful substitute for a collective noun when no other comes immediately to mind, and sounds a little more imaginative than just the word 'stuff'. After Bernadette Devlin's maiden speech in the House of Commons in 1969, she commented on the ritual, 'All this stand up, sit down, kneel down and how's-your-father was so funny.' More recently, the phrase has acquired a sexual connotation as in, with barely concealed innuendo, 'a bit of how's your father'. Similarly, 'hanky panky' has come to mean covert sexual activity, foolish or inadvisable behaviour; that phrase is derived from the magician's mock Latin 'hocus pocus', possibly a parody of *Hoc est corpus*. The word 'hoax' is thought to derive from 'hocus'.

Hue and cry

A noisy commotion over some spot of bother. Until the beginning of the nineteenth century 'hue and cry' was the old legal term for an official outcry made when calling out for assistance, 'with horn and with voice', in the pursuit of a suspected criminal escaping arrest. The phrase must have been in use since the beginning of the last millennium because the Norman French word *huer* means 'to shout'. Thieves failing to respond to the 'hue and cry' were liable to greater penalties once they were caught, hence the increased clamour, and cry of alarm in the case of the villain.

Humble pie, to eat

To make a humble apology or to submit oneself to a certain degree of humiliation, to climb down from a position one has assumed, to be obliged to take a lower station. Here humble is a play on the word 'umble', the umbles being the offal – the heart, liver and entrails – of an animal, usually the deer, considered a delicacy by some, although most thought them only fit for the servants. When the lord of the manor and his family dined on venison at high table, the huntsman and lower orders of the household took lower seats and partook of the umbles made into a pie. James Russell Lowell observed in 1864:

> Disguise it as you will, flavour it as you will, call it what you will, umble pie is umble pie, and nothing else.

I counted them all out and I counted them all back

During the Falklands War of 1982 Brian Hanrahan, a BBC war correspondent with the naval Task Force sent by Britain to recapture the Falkland Islands from Argentina, spoke these carefully considered words in order to report that no aircraft had been shot down during a mission, and so as not to reveal the military secret of the numbers. The Sea Harriers from HMS *Hermes* had just returned from a bombing raid against Argentinian positions at Port Stanley, the capital of the Falklands. The expression, so reassuring to people listening or watching anxiously 8,000 miles away in Britain, became a catchphrase for a time.

I have seen the future and it works

A widely used catchphrase that caught on immediately after it was first coined by American reformer and journalist Lincoln Steffans

(1879–1955), who was inspired by a visit to the Soviet Union and his meeting with Lenin in 1919. The phrase has been reworked by the Orange mobile-telephone company for its slogan 'The future is Orange'.

I'll have what she's having

A line from the 1989 film *When Harry met Sally*, whose central theme is whether a man and a woman can enjoy friendship without sex. The character played by Meg Ryan fakes an orgasm in a coffee bar. Her performance is so realistic that the woman at the next table, when approached by the waiter for her order says, 'I'll have what she's having.'

Imitation is the sincerest form of flattery

However peeved one may be that someone has copied one's style or work, one should keep calm and remember this sage advice and take it as a compliment. This phrase probably dates from the early nineteenth century. In the first century, Lucius Vitellius, father of Aulus Vitellius, Roman Emperor in AD 69, with the help of excessive flattery and general sycophancy made himself in turn a favourite of Tiberius, Caligula, Claudius and Nero. His name became a Roman synonym for one skilled in the art of flattery.

According to Benjamin Disraeli (1804–81):

Everyone likes flattery; and when it comes to Royalty you should lay on with a trowel.

However, heard on television, 'Flattery is the floating cockroach in the milk of human kindness'. It is said that only two groups of people fall for flattery – men and women.

In extremis

To be in dire straits or at the point of death. The phrase is commonly used, probably with some exaggeration, and is Latin for 'in the furthest reaches'.

Insult to injury, to add

To hurt, by word or deed, someone who has already suffered an act of violence or injustice. During the Augustan era, the so-called Golden Age of Latin literature (27 BC–AD 14), Phaedrus translated Aesop's fables into Latin verse, peppering them with anecdotes of his own. He quotes the fable about a bald man who tried to kill a fly that had bitten him on the head, missed the insect and gave his pate a sharp slap. Whereupon the fly said, 'You wished to kill me for a mere touch. What will you do to yourself since you have added insult to injury?'

Iron Chancellor, the

The original Iron Chancellor was Prince Otto von Bismarck (1815–98), the creator of the German Empire. A century later Gordon Brown, Chancellor of the Exchequer in the Labour government elected in 1997, was so called for his characteristic frugality with the nations' budgets, no doubt overseeing the finances with an iron hand, that is, with severe or harsh control.

Iron Lady, the

Even before she became Prime Minister, the then Leader of the Opposition Margaret Thatcher was dubbed the Iron Lady by the Soviet Defence Ministry newspaper *Red Star* in January 1976, in an article accusing her of trying to rekindle the Cold War in what they interpreted as a viciously anti Soviet-speech. She had said, 'The Russians are bent on world dominance . . . the Russians put guns before butter.' She had, in fact, borrowed the phrase from a surprising source – one of the leaders of the Nazi Party. Hermann Goering (1893–1946) made a radio broadcast in 1936 in which he said, 'Guns will make us powerful; butter will only make us fat,' often misquoted as 'guns before butter'. The article mistakenly suggested that she was already known by this nickname in Britain, although Marje Proops had dubbed her 'The Iron Maiden' in the *Daily Mirror* in 1975. An iron maiden was a medieval instrument of torture in the form of a human-figure-shaped box with spiked doors which could be closed mechanically, slowly piercing its victim. Iron Maiden was also the name of a popular heavy-metal group of the 1980s.

Joneses – Keeping up with the Joneses

This phrase defines twentieth-century materialism as the never-ending struggle to keep up appearances, keeping up with the apparent affluence of one's neighbours, paying particular attention to the cars they drive, the holidays they take, the schools their children attend and all sorts of other lifestyle indicators. American Arthur R Momand ('Pop'), whose strip cartoon was first published in the *New York Globe* in 1913, probably invented the phrase. It was based on Momand's own experiences of living beyond his means in a prosperous neighbourhood and his realization that all his neighbours were doing the same as him. The phrase had spread to Britain by the 1940s, where its sentiments remain rampant.

Just when you thought it was safe to go back in the water

Following the worldwide popularity of Stephen Spielberg's epic shark thriller *Jaws* (1975), this phrase was used to promote *Jaws 2* (1978). It was much imitated and parodied, 'Jaws 3, just when you thought it was safe to go to the toilet' was seen as graffiti in London in 1979. Or 'The return of Julian Bream – just when you thought it was safe to go to the lute' (graffito on a poster Amsterdam, 1983). 'Just when you thought . . .' remains a commonly used phrase for headline writers or as an opening gambit in conversation.

Keep it real

This is the cry of contemporary youth and is one of many suburban catchphrases of the increasingly popular television character Ali G, who was asked by Channel 4 to interview a number of public figures for the *Eleven O'Clock Show*. The comic character Ali G is an irreverent Asian 'urban gansta' who comes from Staines – and is played by a white Jewish actor, Sacha Baron Cohen. Other buzz words include, 'booyakasha', and 'risspeck'. He has developed a much-imitated comic patois and describes himself, 'Me look iz South Central LA wiv a twist of Staines'. He now has his own show called *Da Ali G Show*.

Kilroy was here
The motto of the graffiti artist. During the Second World War, the phrase 'Kilroy was here' was found written or scrawled wherever US troops, particularly Air Transport Command, had been. Its origin is a matter of conjecture. One suggestion is that a shipyard inspector, James L Kilroy (d. 1962), at Quincy, Massachussetts, chalked up the words on material he had inspected. It was the title of a film in 1947. Kilroy, whoever he might be, is closely related to the British 'Chad' – drawn as a bald-headed figure with a large nose who appears looking over a wall with the words, 'Wot, no . . .' – the phrase was completed with the word to suit, as a protest or comment on shortages or shortcomings.

Kitchen-sink drama
A type of drama popular in the 1950s in which the plot centres on the more sordid aspects of working-class or lower-middle-class domestic life. Much of the action takes place in the kitchen or at the kitchen sink, which presumably is a metaphor to suggest drudgery and the dullness of dirty dishwater. Plays such as *Look Back in Anger* (1956; this play gave birth to the phrase, 'angry young men') by John Osborne (1929–94) were examples of these types of dramas and used such squalid settings to emphasize their message of protest against the established values of the time. More recently Joanna Trollope's stories of domestic dramas and upheavals feature the lives of the middle-class country set and her books are known as 'Aga sagas', because much of the action takes place near the comfort of this famous stove seen in most country kitchens worth their salt.

Kiss of death
This phrase derives from Judas Iscariot's kiss given to Christ in the Garden of Gethsemane before he betrayed him (Luke 23:48 and Matthew 26:49). Also known as a 'Judas kiss', meaning an insincere act of courtesy or false affection. In Mafia circles, a kiss

from the boss is no sign of affection, but a fatal omen that one's life expectancy is not looking too good. The phrase is often used in political or business contexts meaning that certain associations may not bode well.

Labour isn't working

Saatchi & Saatchi coined this pertinent phrase during the Conservative Party general-election campaign of 1978, and Margaret Thatcher's victory over the governing Labour Party is, in some part, credited to the strength of this play on words. The posters bearing the slogan showed a long queue outside an unemployment office. The sentiments were to ring rather hollow when unemployment continued to rise under the new Tory government.

Labour's double whammy

Another intriguing Saatchi & Saatchi strap-line for the Conservative Party's 1992 election campaign. Posters appeared showing a boxer with two huge boxing gloves with this legend, and the phrase caused considerable national bafflement, although the concept of the 'double whammy' has been well known in the States since the 1950s. Inspired by the 1992 posters, the idiom has gone into common usage. One source suggested that it was fighting talk from the Dick Tracy comic strip, another credited cartoonist Al Capp. Its dictionary meaning is 'a thing with supernatural power, especially bringing bad luck', but it is most likely that the derivation is from the boxing world and means a double blow.

Land fit for heroes, a

The actual phrase was the title of a verse by GK Chesterton (1874–1936) with its cynical undertones:

> They said (when they had dined at Ciro's)
> The land would soon be fit for heroes

And now they've managed to ensure it
For only heroes could endure it.

It was adapted from a semi-official political slogan from the time shortly after the First World War. When the war was over, Prime Minister, David Lloyd George (1863–1945) coined this phrase in a speech at Wolverhampton on 24 November 1918 when he said, 'What is our task? To make Britain a fit country for heroes to live in.' By 1921, with wages falling and a general economic depression, the sentiment was frequently mocked and ridiculed. F Scott Fitzgerald (1896–1940) quipped in *The Crack Up*:

> Show me a hero and I will write you a tragedy.

Land of Nod, the

This was the land to which Cain was exiled after he had slain Abel (Genesis 4:16). The phrase refers to the gentle state of sweet dreams, and to nod off means to go to sleep, obviously derived from the fact that the head tends to fall forward when one feels drowsy. Jonathan Swift, the famous seventeenth-century satirist, (1667–1745), was the first to make the pun on the phrase from Genesis in his little-known work, *Complete Collection of Genteel and Ingenious Conversation* (1731–8) – usually referred to as *Polite Conversation* – in which he wrote that he was 'going to the land of Nod', meaning that he was going to sleep. The phrase has been used in that context ever since.

Legal, decent, honest, truthful

Think what you like about advertising, this is the mission statement of the Advertising Standards Authority. All British advertising should be all the above in order to uphold the essence of good advertising. The organization was founded in 1962 when the slogan was 'Legal, Clean, Honest, Truthful'. The phrase was used as the title of a Radio 4 comedy series about advertising, broadcast in the mid-1980s.

Lemon – The answer's a lemon

Ask a silly question, get a silly answer. This retort means 'no comment'. The phrase is a reasonable answer to an unreasonable or absurd request, or question. The expression probably originated in America at the beginning of the twentieth century, using the various meanings given to the word 'lemon'. The fruit with its sharp juice represents a tart reply to an unreasonable request. To describe something or somebody as a lemon is to mean it, he or she is somehow inadequate – an unattractive person, an unsatisfactory object such as an unreliable car, or a simpleton.

Life begins at forty

Now a rather dated catchphrase taken from the title of a book by the American professor William B Pitkin (1878–1953) published in 1932. The book defined the new-found leisure time that many people discovered they had after forty, and encouraged them to enjoy the second half of their lives, especially by taking up new interests. Jack Yellen and Ted Shapiro wrote a song with this title, and a gutsy rendition of it by singer Sophie Tucker at the age of fifty-three was a huge hit. Nowadays, people want to stay younger for longer and deny their so-called middle age, while economic pressures mean that most people have less spare time to take up new hobbies.

Life's a beach

A colloquial slogan probably originating in Australia in the late 1980s to celebrate the hedonistic lifestyle of sun, sea and surf. The phrase may have been a pun based on the cynical American

expressions, 'Life's a bitch, then you die' or 'Life's a bitch, then you marry one'. In the summer of 1991 the Body Shop devised a clever slogan for suntan products with 'Life's a beach, then you fry', while 'Life's a binge, then you diet' was seen in the *Observer* in 1990.

Lightning never strikes the same place twice

In your dreams. This is a classic case of legend-as-wishful-thinking, for this commonly held belief just doesn't hold water. Many tall buildings and trees have been struck by lightning more than once. The statue of William Penn on City Hall in Philadelphia is struck by lightning about five times every year, and the Empire State Building in New York up to ten times. Nor are humans immune: an American Park Ranger from Virginia, Roy C Sullivan, claims to have been struck on seven different occasions between 1942 and 1977 although he has suffered only relatively minor injuries, but has a collection of singed hats as evidence. Thanks to lightning conductors, invented in 1752 by Benjamin Franklin (1706–90) who, after his famous kite experiment proved that lightning contained an electrical charge, designed a vertical copper rod attached to the top of buildings to earth the electricity and save the building. He fell out with King George III, patron of the Sciences in the eighteenth century, who favoured round lightning conductors.

Long time no see

A mock greeting, or verbal shorthand, originating from the pidgin-English phrases used by the colonial British and Americans in the Far East, dating back to the beginning of the twentieth century and still in use today. The variant 'long time no see, short time buckshee' ('free') was how servicemen dreamt they would be welcomed by their favourite prostitute after a long spell abroad. Expatriates and servicemen imported the phrase and it became well used on both sides of the Atlantic. In similar style, 'Who he?' is another shorthand term, this time from America. Harold Wallace Ross (1892–1951) founded the sophisticated literary magazine the *New Yorker* in 1925 and, with his keen eye for detail and perfection, would write pertinent notes on typescripts, such as 'Hogwash', 'Transcends credulence' or 'Who he?'

Love means never having to say you're sorry

A line taken from the successful 1970 film, *Love Story* by Eric Segal. Ryan O'Neill says it to Ray Milland, playing his father-in-law. He is quoting his student wife (Ali MacGraw) who has just died. Unusually, Segal wrote the novel after the film screenplay, in which the penultimate sentence is 'Love means *not ever* having to say you're sorry'. The phrase was much used and abused in the decade to follow. At the end of the 1972 film *What's Up Doc?* Ryan O'Neal in self-parody quotes the line to his co-star, Barbra Streisand. A graffito from 1974 reads, 'A vasectomy means never having to say you're sorry'.

Lovely jubbly

'Jubbly' is one amongst many euphemisms for money. Jubbly was originally the trade name for an orange drink in the 1950s and 1960s, probably because it rhymes with bubbly, which used the slogan 'Lovely Jubbly'. It came to national prominence with the popularity of the BBC comedy series *Only Fools and Horses*, as it was a catch-all catchphrase of Del Boy, the lovable wide boy played by David Jason. Other slang words for money include 'dosh' possibly derived from the African colonial word for a tip – 'dash'; 'lids' and 'lolly' may have developed from the L or £ symbol for a pound.

Luck – A lorra lorra luck

This phrase has been exaggerated by the woman who first coined it, in self-parody of her pronounced Liverpudlian accent. Cilla Black, singer and presenter of the successful television programme *Blind Date*, wishes her contestants a 'lorra lorra luck', meaning 'good luck', that is, 'a lot of luck', before they play the dating game. She also used the phrase 'a lorra, lorra laffs' when she presented another television show, *Surprise, Surprise*. It is a key phrase used by impressionists.

Mad – As mad as a hatter

A renowned simile ever since Lewis Carroll's (1832–98) *Alice in Wonderland* (1865), although it can be found in WM Thackeray's

(1811–63) *Pendennis* (1850) and is recorded in America as early as 1836. The likely reason for linking hat makers with madness is that hatters used the chemical mercurous nitrate in the making of felt hats, and its side effects can produce trembling symptoms as those suffered in St Vitus's Dance. It is believed that Lewis Carroll based his character on Theophilus Carter, a furniture dealer who was known locally as the 'mad hatter' because he wore a top hat and devised fanciful inventions such as an alarm-clock bed which tips the sleeper to the floor when it's time to wake up. It has also been suggested that the original mad hatter was Robert Crab, a seventeenth-century English eccentric who gave all his belongings to the poor and only ate dock leaves and grass.

Mad – As mad as a March hare

Lewis Carroll also refers to the madness of the March hare in *Alice in Wonderland* because hares run wild in March, the beginning of their rutting season.

> The March hare will be much the most interesting and perhaps, as this is May, it won't be raving mad – at least not so mad as it was in March.

Make do and mend

Official morale-boosting slogan which has a special place in the language for people of a certain age, meaning to make do with what you already have and repair it rather than buying a replacement. It was in common use by 1943 and set the tone for British life during the Second World War, and for many years after

while food and clothing continued to be rationed. It may have derived from 'make and mend', which was a Royal Navy term for an afternoon free from work when the time was spent mending clothes and darning socks. There were even 'make do and mend' departments in stores. The phrase was designed to encourage thrift and the repairing of old garments and furniture rather than buying new and using up scarce resources. This slogan struck a chord in the British psyche, although it seems somewhat quaint to young members of today's consumer society, and the old sentiment to 'waste not, want not' lives on in recycling. Sadly, the art of darning is no more, not least because young Brownies are not taught such skills these days.

Make hay while the sun shines
To act promptly when the opportunity presents itself (see **Carpe diem** and **Strike while the iron's hot**, q.v.). One today is worth two tomorrows, while, as seen on a postcard, 'There's many a lemon dries up unsqueezed'. The phrase originated when many people worked on the land, and appeared in the sixteenth century. 'To make hay' is an old phrase meaning to disorganize and throw things into confusion and disorder. Before the days of the baler hay was tossed about with a pitchfork before being gathered in.

> The sun shines hot, and we use delay,
> Cold biting winter mars our hop'd for hay.
>
> Shakespeare, *Henry V*

I made hay while the sun shone.
My work sold.
Now, if the harvest is over
And the world cold,
Give me the bonus of laughter
As I lose hold.

Sir John Betjeman (1906–84), 'The Last Laugh'

Man – A drowning man will clutch at a straw

Someone in desperate circumstances will reach out and grab hold of anything, however flimsy or inadequate, in the hope of surviving the situation. The phrase is often shortened to 'clutching at straws'. No one is sure of the origin of this unpleasant metaphor, nor of the other well-known drowning phrase and common belief that 'His whole life passes before the eyes of a drowning man'. The word 'straw' has been used as a metaphor for the insubstantial or groundless for hundreds of years, such as a 'man of straw', someone financially insecure or with a poor credit rating; 'the last straw (that broke the camel's back)', that little extra burden which makes something no longer bearable, as with the camel's load, tipping the balance of tolerance. A 'straw in the wind' is a slight hint that suggests much, but in the event, delivers little.

Man – A man's gotta do what a man's gotta do

A macho expression used to emphasize the difficult and dangerous actions a man is forced to take in his life. It may have come from American strip cartoons of the 1930s in this style, and an early example of its literary use appears in John Steinbeck's novel *The Grapes of Wrath* (1939), evoking the Southern American dialect:

I know this – a man got to do what he got to do.

John Wayne first delivered the line on celluloid in the film *Stagecoach* (1939), and it has been paraphrased ever since; or in a play on the words, meaning to show great determination, 'a man's gotta chew what a man's gotta chew'.

Outside the context of the Wild West it is usually used facetiously. Shortly before the Gulf War in 1991 a US truck driver, William J Brown, from Sioux Falls, South Dakota, decided to embark on a one-man peace mission to see Saddam Hussein personally. After the meeting he was quoted in the *Independent*, 'In Sioux Falls a man's got to do what a man's got to do'.

Man – One man's meat is another man's poison

This is a very old adage that has inspired an endless stream of spinoffs and simply means that what is palatable or beneficial to one person is distasteful or harmful to another. The phrase 'different strokes for different folks' pretty well sums up the meaning. The rhythm and phrasing of this expression have given rise to an endless stream of imitations. To an adulterer, perhaps, 'One man's mate is another man's passion' or 'One man's Jill is another man's thrill', or to a vegetarian, 'one man's meat is another man's *poisson*'. 'One man's floor is another man's ceiling' is attributed to D Bloodworth (1967). In ancient times meat and bread were generic terms for food, so in Italy 'bread' stood for food and in Britain, once famous for eating roast meat, the use of the word meat in many proverbs simply meant food.

Man – The man on the Clapham omnibus

The man in the street. This typically ordinary person on the bus was invented by a law lord, Lord Bowen, in 1903. While summing up a case for negligence he told the jury, 'We must ask ourselves what the man on the Clapham omnibus would think.' In those days the omnibus was still a horse-drawn carriage and Clapham was a suburb that the judge obviously regarded as the home of common sense. Clapham is an area of south London that is light-heartedly pronounced 'clarm' because it has attracted many well-heeled, well-spoken residents who have snapped up property there.

Man – The man with the plan

The original man with the plan was the Labour Party leader, Hugh Gaitskell. This was the caption to his picture on general-election campaign posters in 1959, at which his party was defeated. The next man dubbed as such was Jonathan Ross, presenter of a highly successful, anarchic television chat show series in the 1980s.

Man – The man you love to hate

This man was the extravagant Austrian film director Eric von Stroheim (1885–1957) after he appeared as an actor in the First World War propaganda film, *The Heart of Humanity* (1918), in which he played an obnoxious German officer who not only tried to rape the leading lady, but nonchalantly tossed a baby out of a window. The phrase was used to publicize the film and it succeeded in whipping up public emotion. At the film's première in Los Angeles, von Stroheim was booed and jeered at when he appeared on stage. A 1979 film tribute to the work of von Stroheim was entitled *The Man You Love to Hate*. It is now a phrase in general use to describe any alluring or attractive villain.

Man from the Pru, Ask the man from the Pru

The Prudential Assurance Company Ltd was founded in 1848 and the phrase evolved long before the days of direct debit and telephone banking. 'The man from the Pru' was familiar to millions as the man who knocked at the door, to collect life-insurance premiums. It had become a music-hall joke by the end of the nineteenth century, but the phrase did not appear as an official company slogan until after the Second World War, when it was applied to advertisements.

Marie Céleste, Like the Marie Céleste
An eerily quiet and deserted place, somewhere normally occupied, but uncannily empty and quiet. The Mary Céleste was an American brigantine found abandoned, ready to sail, between the Azores and Portugal on 5 December 1872. The ship's one lifeboat, sextant, chronometer, register and crew were missing and no trace of any of them was ever found. It remains one of the unsolved mysteries of the high seas to this day. Hence the use of the ship's name to describe a silent, empty place. Why 'Mary' should be 'Marie' is open to conjecture, but it might be because of its association with the French 'Céleste'.

May the force be with you!
A phrase used to bid farewell, with overtones of a blessing, in the American film Star Wars (1977) by George Lucas, and in its prequels and sequels. The Force is the life force of the universe, the power of good. To millions of the film's fans it is almost the equivalent of 'May God go with you'. More parochially, the Cornish police used it in a recruitment campaign, and President Reagan, always at ease quoting from the movies, used it in a speech about his Star Wars weapons programme, named after the film, saying, 'The force is with us'. Radio disc jockeys are known to repeat it frequently every May the Fourth.

Men stand with their backs to the fire
This expression has no military connotations, as it might suggest at first sight, but has a tenuous link with Noah. This phenomenon is

still observed, for men do seem to like to stand on the hearth rug facing out into the room, perhaps to hold court, in a lord-of-the-manor sort of way. Because open fires are less common these days, this expression is not heard quite so often, but an old explanation is that when the dog's nose proved to be too small to plug a leak in Noah's Ark, Noah sat on the hole to keep the water out. Ever since it has been observed that men seem to need to warm their backs and dogs have cold wet noses.

Mentioned in dispatches
To single out someone for particular congratulation or recommendation for carrying out a task with distinction. Dispatches are official communications sent or dispatched to the relevant government ministries from commanding officers during a military campaign. If an officer is listed or mentioned in British naval, army or air force dispatches commending his or her conduct in action, he or she is entitled to wear a small bronze oak leaf on the left breast or upon the medal ribbon for that particular campaign.

Milk has gotta a lotta bottle
Milk was remarketed as a macho drink, not just for kids, in 1985 with this fighting phrase. The word bottle denotes courage or guts and has been used in this sense since the late 1940s. To 'bottle out' or to 'lose one's bottle' means to shrink from. One suggestion is that bottle comes from Cockney rhyming slang, either 'bottle and glass' – arse; or 'bottle of beer' – fear; or 'bottle and glass' – class. The associations between either arse, fear or class with courage are not obvious, but links can be guessed at. Arse meaning bottom, which if you have a lot of you are brave; fear to mean provoking fear in others; or class which a boxer has; while if he loses it he has lost his bottle. Cockney slang was used increasingly during the 1970s, with the influence of numerous television crime dramas such as *The Sweeney* and *Minder*.

Miss is as good as a mile, a

Coming second is just not good enough. A failure is a failure by however small a margin. Conversely, though, a narrow escape is an escape. An old form of the phrase was 'an inch in a miss is as good as an ell'. An 'English ell' was an old unit of measurement equal to forty-five inches. Another old saying is 'give him an inch and he'll take an ell'; the 'ell' later evolved into 'mile'. It has also been said that 'a miss is as good as her smile'.

Miss Otis regrets

A very handy excuse in replying to an invitation to a function that one does not wish to accept. It originated in Cole Porter's 1934 song of the same name, in which Miss Otis's butler, with sublime understatement, gives his mistress's tragic reason for not being able to keep a lunch date. After being scorned by her lover, she has been hanged for his murder.

> She drew her forty-four pistol and shot the dirty rascal down,
> Now Old Lady Otis regrets she's disabled and can't lunch today.

Moon – To bay at the moon

'To bay, or bark, at the moon' is to crave for what is unattainable. This fanciful phrase means to fluster about pointlessly, aiming at something or some idea probably out of reach. It can be said of children with big ideas that they might 'cry for the moon to play with'. But a deranged dog may think he can frighten the moon by baying at it. It is an old superstition that when a dog howls at the moon it's an ill omen of death or bad luck.

Moon – To shoot the moon

This is an American expression meaning to leave without paying one's bills or rent, or to remove swiftly one's household goods under cover of night to avoid their seizure by a landlord or creditor, more colloquially known as 'to do a moonlight flit' and often shortened to 'do a moonlight'. Simply to 'moonlight' means to take a second job supposedly at night to supplement one's wages from the day job. References to the moon are often used to denote that something is fanciful: for instance, unrealistic ideas are known as 'moonshine'; 'to cry for the moon', mentioned above, means to crave for what is totally beyond one's reach. *Shoot the Moon* was the title of the 1981 Alan Parker film about a well-heeled family who split up.

Mother of all battles, the

This phrase entered the English language thanks to Saddam Hussein, Iraqi president since 1979. In 1990 Saddam invaded Kuwait and was repulsed by a coalition of Western and Arab forces during the Gulf War. Just before the beginning of Allied attacks in 1991 Saddam pronounced:

> The devil Bush and his treacherous gang, with criminal Zionism, have begun the great showdown, the mother of all battles between good and evil.
>
> Speech in Baghdad, 6 January, describing Operation Desert Storm. Quoted in the *Sunday Times*, 27 January 1991

The phrase has been adapted to describe something terrible or arduous and is used in such contexts as 'the mother of all rows'. Expressions such as 'the mother and father of all hangovers' were, however, commonly used in the English language well before the Gulf War.

Muster, to pass

To come up to an adequate standard, to pass inspection or to get by. Originally 'muster' was a military term for the gathering of soldiers for inspection. To 'muster in' means to enrol, and to 'muster out' means that the group disperses or falls out.

My old Dutch

A colloquial term for a wife or, nowadays, long-term female partner. Although Dutch in English expressions often refers to a person or thing from Holland, or, especially in America, from Germany (as a corruption of *Deutsch*, German), in this instance the word is a contraction of 'duchess'. Cockney rhyming slang has it that wife is 'Duchess of Fife', shortened to 'Dutch'. The expression gained currency notably among Cockneys and costermongers from the late Victorian and early Edwardian music halls, and especially from the song 'My Old Dutch' performed by Albert Chevalier (1861–1923), the 'costers' laureate' known as Albert the Great, who was enormously popular in his day.

Nail – on the nail

This is a very old phrase meaning to pay immediately or on the spot and generally it means now, at once. In medieval times, a nail was a shallow vessel mounted on a post or stand and business deals were closed by payments placed in the 'nail'. It may have been so named from the resemblance of the stand to the shape of a nail. Outside the Bristol Corn Exchange such nails can still be seen in the form of four bronze pillars and it is said that if a buyer was satisfied with the sample of grain shown on the nail he paid on the spot. However, there could be another derivation for this phrase from the world of wine tasting. Latin for 'on the nail' is *supernaculum*, and this word also describes the very best wine, meaning that the wine is so fine that the imbiber only leaves enough in the glass to make a bead on a nail. And the French say of first-class wine, *faire rubis sur l'ongle* – 'to make a ruby on the nail'. Thomas Nash (1567–1601) in *Pierce Penilesse* (1592) wrote that after a man had drunk from his glass it was customary to turn the cup upside down and let a drop fall on the thumbnail. If the drip rolled off the drinker was obliged to fill up and drink again, eventually ending up 'on the floor'.

Nail – another nail in the coffin

A depressing phrase which is applied to a further event in a situation that is getting progressively worse; one more factor to plunge a person into greater disfavour, to hasten his dismissal, or downfall, or death. The final nail can be compared with the 'last straw' (see **Man – A drowning man will clutch at a straw**, q.v.). Peter Pindar (Dr J Wolcot, 1738–1819) wrote in one of his *Expostulary Odes*:

> Care to our coffin adds a nail, no doubt.

The phrase came to be adopted by smokers – who, as early as the 1920s, referred to cigarettes as 'coffin nails' – becoming a stock response as someone accepted yet another cigarette. At the time, however, they were referring to the hazards of a smoker's cough. The links between smoking and cancer, and smoking and heart disease were recognized later (when cigarettes earned another nickname – 'cancer sticks').

Nation of shopkeepers

This was meant as an insult to the English people by Napoleon Bonaparte (1769–1821), who said 'L'Angleterre est une nation de boutiquiers', which he must have read in Adam Smith's *The Wealth of Nations* (1776):

> To found a great empire for the sole purpose of raising up a people of customers, may at first sight appear a project fit only for a nation of shop keepers.

Nation shall speak peace unto nation

The motto of the BBC from 1927 was put forward by Dr Montague John Rendall (1862–1950), a schoolmaster who became one of the first five governors when the original company was incorporated and its coat of arms created. The words echo a passage in Micah 4:3: 'Nation shall not lift up a sword against nation'. In 1932, however, it was decided that the BBC's mission was not principally to broadcast to other nations, but to provide a service for a home and colonial audience. A new assertion was introduced by Dr Rendall – *Quaecunque* – 'Whatsoever' – when the new BBC headquarters at Broadcasting House in London was built, which reflected the spirit of the passage from Philippians 4:8: 'Whatsoever things are beautiful and honest and of good report'. In 1948, however, the BBC reverted to its first motto after its vital role in international broadcasting during the Second World War.

Naughty but nice

Between 1981 and 1984 the National Dairy Council used this alliterative and somewhat suggestive slogan in a campaign to promote fresh cream cakes. The novelist Salman Rushdie claimed to have created the phrase when he was the castaway on BBC's *Desert Island Discs*. Before achieving fame and fatwa Rushdie had been an advertising copywriter in London, but his claim was refuted by others who had worked on the account. The phrase was certainly not original, as it was the title for a 1939 film about a classical-music professor who accidentally wrote a popular song, starring Dick Powell and Ronald Reagan. It has also been an oblique phrase implying sexual intercourse since about 1900.

Necessity is the mother of invention

An imperative need will force one to summon extra creative forces to devise a solution, or to create something, to alleviate a problem. The phrase was probably first coined by Plato in the fourth century BC in *The Republic*. More modern derivations of the phrase are 'A guilty conscience is the mother of invention' and 'Boredom is the mother of invention'. And in a chiastic twist by one Thorstein Veblen (1857–1929), 'Invention is the mother of necessity'.

However, Daniel Defoe (1661?–1731) wrote in *Serious Reflections of Robinson Crusoe*:

> Necessity makes an honest man a knave.

Never knowingly undersold

The motto of the John Lewis stores since the 1930s. The founder of the John Lewis Partnership, John Spedan Lewis, formulated this line in about 1920 to declare the pricing policy which began with his father, John Lewis, who first opened a small shop in London's Oxford Street in 1864. It is thought that the slogan was used internally before it was given public expression in the 1930s with the promise, 'If you can buy more cheaply elsewhere anything you have just bought from us we will refund the difference.' 'Never knowingly undersold' still appears on carrier bags and on the sides of delivery vehicles and the 'If you can buy . . .' undertaking is printed on the reverse of sales bills. The firm does not advertise and the phrase has an almost mystical significance for the partnership. It is a tortuous phrase that requires some thought to work out its meaning.

News – No news is good news

The absence of information justifies continued optimism; that is, if all's quiet, then there is no cause for alarm. The phrase probably dates back to the early seventeenth century, and can be explained by Plutarch's phrase in about 100 AD that 'Bad news travels fast'.

> For evil news rides post, while good news baits.
> John Milton (1608–1674), *Samson Agonistes*

The word news, now understood as a singular noun, was still plural up to the nineteenth century:

> The news from Austria are very sad, and make one very anxious.
> Letter from Queen Victoria to the King of the Belgians,
> 20 August 1861

The word is short for 'new stories', and the old spelling was 'newes', a literal translation from the French *nouvelles*. (Seen as graffiti: 'No nukes is good nukes'.)

Nice one Cyril!

This enormously popular catchphrase was an advertising slogan that struck a chord with the public, who dropped it as quickly as they had embraced it. The line first appeared in a television commercial for Wonderloaf bread in 1972, written by Peter Mayle (author of *A Year in Provence*). Why the phrase was so popular is a mystery. It had a Cockney mateyness, it was fun to say and it could be applied to all sorts of situations, not least sexual ones. In 1973 it was chanted by Tottenham Hotspur football supporters who were fans of player Cyril Knowles, and who went as far as recording a song about him. The comedian Cyril Fletcher used it as the title to his 1978 autobiography. Suddenly the phrase became old hat and it did not make another public appearance until it was used on posters in 1989 advertising Access credit cards. It showed the corpulent figure of the politician, Sir Cyril Smith (1928–), trying to touch his toes.

Nineteenth hole, the

The bar at the golf clubhouse. The standard course has eighteen holes so the player who has played badly can drown his sorrows at the nineteenth. The term was first heard by American golfers in the 1920s.

Not my bag

A slang expression for something which is definitely not one's subject or style. It probably came from the American jazz scene, 'bag' meaning a personal style of playing; for instance, 'playing with a hip-hop band was not his bag'. This phrase came into general use, being applied to almost anything, in both America and Britain.

Not on your Nellie!

Not bloody likely, not on any account, on your life. One conjecture is that it derives from Cockney rhyming slang from around the 1930s, 'Nellie Duff'; 'duff' rhymes with puff, i.e. breath, that which keeps you alive. Another theory is that your 'nellie' is your stomach, your 'Aunt Nellie' – belly, something that in a more refined age you did not reveal to the world. The phrase was one of comedian Frankie Howerd's (1917–1992) catchphrases, which he popularized in the 1940s. Howerd referred to his many catchphrases as 'verbal punctuation marks' and his camp humour derived from the implied suggestiveness in his emphasis on certain syllables.

Not worth a tinker's damn
This is one of many phrases meaning that something is worthless. Tinkers were itinerant menders of kettles and pans and were a common sight on the streets in the eighteenth century. It has been suggested that the term comes from the tinker's custom of blocking up a hole in the article he was mending with a pellet of bread, thus making a 'dam', or plug, that would hold the molten solder. This pellet was discarded as unreusable when the job was finished. So a tinker's dam is a useless or negligible thing. However, the present spelling of 'damn' alludes to its meaning as a curse or oath, and the phrase is also heard as 'not worth a tinker's cuss', a cuss being slang for a curse. It can only be assumed that tinkers made such a bodged job of their repairs that they frequently uttered oaths of frustration at their own incompetence. It is still common 'to tinker about' with something, which means to fiddle in a clumsy fashion in an attempt to make repairs.

Nudge nudge, wink wink, say no more
A catchphrase understood by everyone during the 1970s, which came from the television comedy show *Monty Python's Flying Circus*, broadcast between 1969 and 1974. Laden with sexual innuendo, these words provided the accompaniment to rhetorical questions such as 'Is your wife a goer, then, eh, eh?' asked by a lewd character played by Eric Idle in a ridiculously suggestive manner, accompanied by much elbow jerking, embarrassed twitching and prodding.

Oil on troubled waters, to pour
A well-known metaphor meaning to mollify or soothe with gentle words, or to use tact and diplomacy to restore calm after an angry or bitter argument. It has been a well-known scientific fact since the first century AD that rough waves are calmed when oil is poured

upon them. According to the Venerable Bede's (673–735) *History of the English Church and People* (731) St Aidan, an Irish monk of Iona, knew of this 'miracle' and gave a young priest a vessel of holy oil to pour on the sea when the waves became stormy on a voyage to fetch a maiden destined to be the bride of King Oswy. On his many Atlantic crossings between Pennsylvania and Portsmouth in the eighteenth century, the ever curious Benjamin Franklin (1706–90) observed not only the Gulf Stream, but also the calming effect of oil on the waves.

Old – As old as Methuselah
This means to be very old indeed. Methuselah is the oldest man referred to in the Bible, and it is written in Genesis (5:27) that he died at the impossibly great age of 969 years. 'As old as the hills' is probably a more realistic simile as hills are indeed extremely ancient features of the landscape.

Old Grey Whistle test, the
In Tin Pan Alley, the popular music-publishing district of New York around 14th Street, and in London's Denmark Street, off Charing Cross Road, songwriters would play their newly penned tunes to the 'old greys' – the elderly doorkeepers and clerks in the offices of music publishers. If the 'old greys' were still whistling the songs after few days, they might be worth publishing. It later became the title of a long-running rock-music programme on BBC television during the 1970s and 1980s.

Old-boy network
This is the art of using one's social connections to get on in life. To arrange something on the old-boy network is to fix it through a social contact or someone from one's old school, instead of through

less nepotistic channels. An old boy or old girl is a former pupil of a particular school, hence old boys' or old girls' societies through which former pupils reunite and reminisce about old times. The old-school tie worn by former pupils of the public and grammar schools is a distinguishing mark, recognized by members of the same privileged class. Nowadays, the practice of 'networking' in order to make contacts is referred to, describing going out to meet people in a similar field who can help advance one in business; that is, meeting those more successful than yourself in the hope that some of their success might rub off.

Once bitten, twice shy
A phrase meaning that one learns from previous experience. Having been caught out once, one is wary or cautious the next time, and you should therefore learn from your mistakes. 'He that stumbles twice at the same stone deserves to have his shins broke', appears in R Taverner's list of *Proverbs and Adages* of 1539 while the American humorist Josh Billings (1818–95) said that 'nobody but a fool gets bit twice by the same dog.'

> I'll trust by leisure him that mocks me once.
> Shakespeare, *Titus Andronicus* (1590)

One sandwich short of a picnic
A derogatory description of someone who is not terribly bright. It is one of many such almost cartoon-like expressions, such as 'one prawn short of a cocktail' and other variations. 'The lights are on but on one's at home' and 'the lift doesn't go to the top floor' have very much the same meaning.

Out for the count
Said of someone who is fast asleep, dead drunk or completely demoralized. It is a boxing and wrestling term meaning to be defeated by being counted out by the referee. If a fighter is floored and does not find his feet within ten seconds counted out loud he has lost the bout, much to the excitement of the audience, who usually raucously accompany the referee while he counts down the seconds. To say 'count me out' means 'do not include me in this.'

Over a barrel

To be stuck in a helpless position, powerless to get yourself out of it, or to be at someone's mercy. The phrase is probably nautical in origin and is said to derive from the practice of draping over a barrel someone who has been rescued from the water when close to drowning, so encouraging the ejection of water from the lungs. A more likely derivation, however, may be a form of punishment or torture in which the victim is bent over a barrel and beaten.

Over the top

An expression that describes something that goes way beyond the bounds of good taste or good sense, or which is outrageously inappropriate. It came from the trenches of the First World War when soldiers were described as going 'over the top' when they scrambled out of the trenches to attack the enemy. *Over The Top* was the name of a bawdy television show in the 1980s, which became known only by its initials, OTT, which are still used in many colloquial contexts. For example, a particularly impassioned verbal outburst, or a person who behaves or dresses outrageously, might be described as OTT.

Oyster – Never eat an oyster unless there's an R in the month

An old maxim that served as sensible advice to avoid the eating of native oysters in the months of May, June, July and August. In the days before modern refrigeration oysters did offer the risk of food poisoning in the warm summer breeding months, which happen not to have an R in their names. Now oysters can be eaten all year round, although normal marketing in Britain still takes place from September to April. As Richard Buttes advised in *Diet's Dry Dinner* (1599):

> The oyster is unseasonable and unwholesome in all months that have not the letter R in their name.

To cheat the rule, people used to eat oysters in August by spelling it 'Orgust'.

Paint the town red, to

To go out and party, to let your hair down and enjoy an uninhibited celebration, to trip the light fantastic, perhaps even to cause some disturbance in town. This phrase of American origin possibly originally alludes to a town's red-light district; that is, the area where prostitutes ply their trade, advertising with a red light in the window of their brothels, and where the cowboys might begin the evening before later extending the party to the rest of town.

Pandora's Box

This is a troublesome 'can of worms' – a gift that seems of great value but is actually a curse, generating all sorts of unmanageable problems. The name Pandora means 'all gifted', because in Greek mythology the gods endowed her with powers which could bring about the ruin of man. Pandora was sent by Zeus as a gift to Epimetheus, who married her, against the advice of his brother Prometheus. She brought with her a large jar – Pandora's box – but, when Epimetheus opened it, all the evils escaped, to afflict the world for ever, while the blessings were lost to mankind. According to some, hope was the last thing that flew out; others believe that hope alone remained in the box. The more modern phrase 'to open a can of worms', which was first used in America in the 1950s, is a euphemism that became popular in the UK in the 1970s. It is a graphic metaphor for a tangled, squirming, unpleasant, or uncontrollable situation that had not been apparent beforehand.

Pavlovian, a Pavlovian response
This sort of response is an automatic reaction made unthinkingly or under the influence of others, and should not be confused with a fluffy meringue cake with summer fruit and whipped cream which was named after the graceful Russian ballet dancer Anna Pavlova (1881–1931). The Russian psychologist Ivan Petrovich Pavlov (1849–1936) pioneered studies into animal behaviour and discovered the conditioned reflex. In his classic experiment he rang a bell before feeding a hungry dog and showed that, after a time, the dog would salivate on hearing the bell even when there was no sight of food. He called this reaction 'psychic salivation' and the phenomenon became known as the conditioned reflex. Dogs were Pavlov's main focus of experiment but he also used monkeys and mice, demonstrating that the conditioned reflex occurs in all animals, including humans, and can be activated by almost any suggestion or environmental factor. One of Pavlov's less successful ventures, however, was his failed attempt to market an appetite stimulant for humans based on dogs' saliva.

Peace in our time
The most vacuous slogan in the run-up to the Second World War were these words, announced by Prime Minister Neville Chamberlain on 30 September 1938 when he returned from signing the Munich agreement with Hitler, hoping that his concession, which effectively abandoned Czechoslovakia to Nazi domination, would pave the way for peace. Despite any personal misgivings he may have had, he experienced vehement opposition to his declaration to the crowds outside Number 10 Downing Street:

> My good friends, this is the second time in our history that there has come back from Germany to Downing Street peace with honour. I believe it is peace for our time. Go home and get a quiet night's sleep.

According to John Colville in *Footprints in Time* (1976), it was Chamberlain's wife who actually persuaded him to use the phrase, which in fact was 'Peace for [not 'in'] our time'. Noël Coward entitled his 1947 play, hypothetically about England after the Germans had conquered, *Peace in Our Time*. Use of the phrase was probably inspired by the Book of Common Prayer:

> Give peace in our time, O Lord.
>
> Morning Prayer, Versicle

Pete – For Pete's sake

An exclamation of annoyance or impatience. Just who Pete is remains a mystery. The expression is perhaps an oath in the name of St Peter; alternatively it may have evolved from 'for pity's sake'. Nowadays, however, this particular curse is not so frequently heard because the threshold of acceptability for far more blasphemous expletives is far lower.

Pig in a poke, a

To buy a pig in a poke is to buy something sight unseen, to make a blind purchase, usually worthless. This is an ancient form of trickery when animals were traded at market and a small suckling pig was taken for sale in a 'poke', a word shortened from the word 'pocket', which was a stout sack. However, people used to try and palm off the runts of the litter to unsuspecting buyers, and even cats were substituted for pigs. The sale had to be agreed without opening the poke for fear of the lively piglet escaping. If the less gullible purchaser insisted on seeing the contents of the poke the salesman might literally have to 'let the cat out of the bag' (hence that other well-known expression), and the game was up. This form of dodgy market trading has been around for hundreds of years, and is referred to in Thomas Tusser's *Five Hundred Good*

Pointes of Husbandrie (1580). The practice was obviously widespread because other languages have similar expressions, such as the French *chat en poche*, which also refer to the folly of buying something without seeing it first. The Latin proverb *caveat emptor* – let the buyer beware – has a similar meaning.

Pile it high, sell it cheap

This golden rule of Tesco Supermarkets was invented by the company founder, Sir John Cohen (1898–1979). It may have been adapted from the American phrase, 'Stack it high, Watch 'em buy', and is still applied in markets today.

Piper – He who pays the piper may call the tune

Whoever pays the bill commands control of the situation. Although this proverb appeared in the seventeenth century, it probably comes from the story, dating from 1284, of the Pied Piper, who didn't get paid, and might be derived from the phrase, 'Who's to pay the piper?' The Pied Piper was an itinerant musician who agreed to rid the town of Hamelin in Westphalia of an infestation of rats and mice. After he had had completed the task his payment was withheld, however, so he led all the town's children away to a mountain cave where they all disappeared. Another possible derivation goes back to the pipers who used to amuse guests at inns or on village greens, and expected to be paid for their efforts. 'Pay' means to discharge a debt and is derived via the French *paier* from the Latin *pax*, peace, from *pacare*, to appease.

Plain as a pikestaff, as

This alliterative phrase originated in the mid-sixteenth century and means that something is perfectly clear, obvious, unambiguous or unmistakable, although its original meaning was bare or unadorned. A pike is a weapon with a long wooden shaft and a pointed steel or iron head, and was used by the military preceding the bayonet. It later came to mean simply a walking stick, especially one used by pilgrims and travellers. The earlier word for 'pikestaff' was 'packstaff', which was the pole on which a peddler carried his pack and which, through many years of use, was worn smooth and plain – hence the original meaning of unadorned.

Pleased as Punch, as

In the traditional comic puppet show *Punch and Judy*, the pompous Mr Punch gloats smugly at the success of his evil actions and superiority over his shrewish wife Judy. The name Mr Punch probably comes from the Italian *pulcinello* (young chicken), and the show was know as *Punchinello* when it first came to England at about the time of the Restoration in 1660. The present scenario is probably similar to the original by the Italian comedian Silvio Fiorello, dating from about 1600. Although the basic plot varies, it usually involves Punch's enraged bludgeoning of his wife, Judy, their child, and several lesser characters, followed by his imprisonment and escape. Often accompanied by his dog, Toby, Punch is a hook-nosed, long-chinned hunchback whose quick wit is triumphant even over the devil. The violence of the storylines is counteracted by slapstick action and comic dialogue. The British humorous magazine *Punch* was founded in 1841, and the character of Punch is still used as its symbol.

Point blank, to ask something

To ask a direct question. This is a sixteenth-century phrase from the sport of archery. The targets had a white, or *blanc* in French, central spot, so the arrows were pointed at the white, that is *point blanc*. In military, and especially artillery, usage, point blank is a range at which there is no fall of shot due to gravity – in other words, a very close range. Any projectile from a firearm 'drops' from the point of aim as the range increases, which in turn means that the further the target, the higher the weapon has to be aimed above it.

Post early for Christmas

This enduring advice from the Post Office probably dates from the 1880s. The aim of the message is to reduce the pressure on the postal system before the Christmas rush of cards and parcels. 'Post early' was a maxim used in the 1920s throughout the year to

encourage letters to be posted early in the day for deliveries to be made later the same day. During the Second World War the phrase was adapted to 'Post early – Before noon'.

Powder – To keep one's powder dry
To be prepared for action, but to be cautious, yet alert; to preserve one's resources. The phrase comes from a saying attributed to Oliver Cromwell (1599–1658), and the powder is, of course, gunpowder. During his cold-blooded and savage Irish campaign of 1649 he is said to have concluded a speech to his troops, who were about to cross the River Slaney before attacking Wexford, with the rousing words, 'Put your trust in God, my boys, and keep your powder dry.' However, it seems likely that the phrase was coined later by the Anglo-Indian soldier Valentine Blacker (1738–1823) and gained the Cromwell attribution through being quoted in 'Oliver's Advice' in E Hayes's *Ballads of Ireland* (1856).

Power to the people
This is the motto of the Black Panther movement in America and dates from 1969. Traditionally shouted with a clenched fist raised, it was publicized by the Black Panther leader, Bobby Seale, in Oakland, California, in July 1969. The Black Panthers were a militant organization notorious for their violent demonstrations and dramatic shootouts with police. It was used by other dissident groups, as Black, White and Red Power were taken up by various other revolutionary organizations. In the revolutionary spirit of the time, John Lennon penned the song 'Power to the People' in 1971.

Pride goes before a fall
An ancient warning for the arrogant to avoid conceit; do not be too cocksure or big-headed, because events may conspire to bring you down. The phrase is shortened from the passage in Proverbs (16:18):

> Pride goeth before destruction,
> and an haughty spirit before a fall.

'Pride goes before, and shame comes after' is another form of the proverb as it was used in the sixteenth and seventeenth centuries.

It has also been said that 'He who gets too big for his britches gets exposed in the end.'

Probably the best lager in the world
In 1973 Orson Welles' mellifluous tones graced the voice-over to this landmark television commercial for Carlsberg lager. The use of the reservation, 'probably', struck an ironic chord in an otherwise gross exaggeration for a very middle-of-the-road product.

Put a sock in it!

A plea to be quiet, to shut up, to make less noise. It comes from the end of the nineteenth and beginning of the twentieth centuries, when the early gramophones, or 'phonographs', had large horns through which the sound was amplified. These mechanical contraptions had no volume controls, and so a convenient method of reducing the volume was to stuff a woollen sock inside the horn.

Queer Street, to be in
Not to be confused with the gay part of town, this phrase means to be in financial difficulties, in dire straits, or in another thoroughfare, Carey Street (see also **Beam ends**, q.v.). Use of the word 'queer' could be a pun on 'query' because Victorian tradesmen might mark the name of customer with a poor credit rating on the ledger with a question mark. It is more likely, however, that it is a direct translation of the German word *querstrasse*, that is, a road at right angles to the main road. Similarly, to be in Carey Street is to be bankrupt. Carey Street is situated in the City of London off Chancery Lane, and is home to the bankruptcy courts. As an aside, to be in a street, metaphorically, is a neat turn of phrase to evoke an emotional state; for instance, in Elvis Presley's (1935–77) first hit song (1955), 'Heartbreak Hotel' lies 'down at the end of Lonely Street'.

Rabbit – Little rabbits have big ears

A twentieth-century Australian modification of the old proverb 'little pitchers have great ears'. It means that grownups should watch their language when talking in front of small children, who often pick up many a hint that the speaker might wish to pass unnoticed. The 'ear' of a pitcher is the handle, which is often ear shaped, and the phrase 'Asses as well as pitchers have big ears' is also common.

Rabbit – More rabbit than Sainsbury's

Said of someone who is thought to waffle on, or to talk pointlessly. 'To rabbit' means to talk and is thought to come from Cockney rhyming slang 'rabbit and pork'. The singers Chas and Dave gave us the line 'rabbit, rabbit', in a song that accompanied one of a series of TV commercials for Courage Best Bitter in Britain in the early 1980s. The advertisement pokes fun at talkative women who interrupt the pleasures of supping pints of beer. However, according to the *Oxford English Dictionary*, the term to rabbit may come from a French dialect word, *rabotte*, meaning to waffle.

Ragtag and bobtail

The riff-raff, the rabble, otherwise known as the 'great unwashed'; all derogatory terms for the masses or lower classes. This expression was common in the sixteenth and seventeenth centuries as 'the rag and tag'. Rags are tatters or remnants of cloth or clothes, and a ruffian or vagabond is still known as a ragamuffin; a muffin was a colloquial diminutive for a pitiful creature. Rag, Tag and Bobtail were popular characters in the early days of children's television in the 1950s; they appeared on the BBC's *Watch with Mother*, and were contemporaries of Andy Pandy and the Flowerpot Men.

Rain check, to take a

A rain check is the receipt or counterfoil of a baseball ticket that can be used at a later date if a game has been interrupted by rain. It is an American expression and the phrase retains the American spelling of 'cheque'. The phrase is now often used, figuratively, to accept an invitation, put it on hold and defer it until a later date. It is, in fact, a polite way of postponing something indefinitely, with only a minor commitment to rearrange.

Real McCoy, the

This is a common American expression, although it probably originated in Scotland in the 1880s, when it was applied to MacKay whisky. This particular brand of whisky was exported to America and Canada, where people of Scottish origin drank it and kept the phrase alive. In the 1890s, however, there is no doubt that it was applied to a famous boxer, the prize fighter Kid 'the Real' McCoy (1872–1940), and this is the spelling that has remained in use. Coca-Cola, probably the most advertised product in the world, adapted the phrase in the 1970s by describing their product as the 'real thing' in comparison with any rival products.

Red – To see red

To give way to excessive passion or anger, or to be violently moved; to indulge in physical violence while in a state of frenzy. The reference is to the Spanish spectacle of bullfighting and the art of taunting the bull. The phrase 'like a red rag to a bull' is said of anything that is calculated to excite rage. Toreadors' capes are lined with red, although there is no evidence that the colour itself incenses the bulls. Red is one of the primary colours and is the colour of passion; it signifies magnanimity and fortitude in heraldry, and in popular folklore it is the colour of magic. Nowadays it is also the colour of revolution or anarchy, although in the nineteenth century, Lord Tennyson (1809–1892) presaged this when he referred to 'Red ruin, and the breaking up of laws' in 'Guinevere'. Red is the colour of the royal livery, and it is said that it was adopted by huntsmen because foxhunting was a royal sport from the time of Henry II (1154–89).

Revenge is a dish best served cold
Be patient, vengeance will be all the more satisfying if you take your time in getting back at someone. It is said that revenge is sweet, but not when you're on the receiving end. There is an old proverb from 1578 that advises, 'Living well is the best revenge', and according to Euripedes (480–406 BC), 'There's nothing like the sight of an old enemy down on his luck.' When it comes to marital revenge, 'When a man steals your wife, there is no better revenge than to let him keep her,' as Sasha Guitry wrote in *Elle et Toi*.

Revenons à nos moutons

A French phrase that means literally 'Let us return to our sheep,' which has been used for hundreds of years in English to mean, 'Let's get back to the subject'. It comes from the French comedy *La Farce de Maistre Pierre Pathelin*; or *l'Avocat Pathelin* (c. 1460), in which a woollen draper accuses a shepherd, Aignelet, of cruelty to his sheep. In telling his story the draper continually digresses from the subject in order to discredit the defendant's attorney, Pierre Pathelin. The judge has to interrupt him continuously by saying 'Mais, mon ami, revenons a nos moutons.' The phrase was frequently quoted by Rabelais (c. 1495–1553) and has a facetious equivalent among some English speakers, when asking someone to keep to the subject, in 'Let's return to our muttons.'

Ride, to be taken for a
This colloquial phrase can be interpreted in one of two ways. It refers either to the victim of a light-hearted joke or prank or, in its sinister and probably original meaning – a completely genuine use of the phrase – to someone who is taken for a ride somewhere and does not come back in one piece, if at all. The rival underworld gangs of American cities in the 1920s and 1930s were virtually at

war with each other, and any unfortunate who was unlucky enough to tempt the wrath of the gang leader, or Don in the case of the Mafia, would be literally taken for a ride in a limousine, ostensibly to discuss certain matters or sort out some misunderstanding. He would be very unlikely to return alive, however.

Riot act, to read the
Figuratively, 'to read the riot act' is to attempt to quell chattering and general commotion or misbehaviour, particularly in a group of children, by vigorous and forceful pleas coupled with threats of the consequences if order is not resumed. The original Riot Act became law in 1715, and stated that when twelve or more people were gathered with the intention of rioting, it was the duty of the magistrates to command them to disperse, and that anyone who continued to riot for one hour afterwards was guilty of a serious criminal offence. It was not superseded until 1986 when the Public Order Act was introduced. 'To run riot' was originally said of hounds that had lost the scent, and was later applied to any group that behaved in a disorderly or unrestrained way.

Roaring Forties, the
A mariner's term for the stormy regions between the southern latitudes 40° and 50°, famous for the prevailing westerly winds. In the days of sail these winds often encouraged mariners to return to Europe via Cape Horn, the southernmost tip of South America (named after a Dutch sailor from the town of Hoorn in Holland in about 1616), instead of the Cape of Good Hope, the southernmost tip of Africa (which was first known as the  Cape of Storms until 1486, when King John II of Portugal ordered the adoption of its present more encouraging name). The term has also been applied to the North Atlantic crossing between the same northern latitudes. On a different tack, the 1920s were known as the 'Roaring Twenties', to reflect the buoyant and upbeat mood which took hold as people sought to obliterate the memory of the horrors of the First World War (see **Bright youngs things**, q.v.).

Rock 'n' roll – It's only rock 'n' roll

Rock and roll was the pop-music style of the latter half of the 1950s, and was an easy-listening form of rhythm and blues with a heavily accented beat and simple repeated phrasing. It became the accompaniment to a youth rebellion and the parental and establishment shock that went with it. The phrase itself was used from about 1953 by the American disc jockey Alan Freed as a racially acceptable term for 'rhythm and blues', which was essentially black music. Its fans were known as 'rockers' and belonged to the era of the 'teddy boy', so called because of their Edwardian style of dress,  after King Edward VII (1841–1910). 'It's only rock 'n' roll' became an ubiquitous graffito in the 1970s after the Rolling Stones album of the same name. In 1977, the punk poet Ian Dury (1942–2000) coined and put to music the much used phrase that summed up the attitude of most rock 'n' rollers, and probably still does, 'sex and drugs and rock 'n' roll'. The term 'rock 'n' roll' was originally American black slang for sexual intercourse.

Rome – To fiddle while Rome burns

To delay or vacillate or do nothing during an emergency or crisis, an allusion to Nero's reputed behaviour during the burning of Rome in AD 64. Nero Claudius Caesar (AD 37–68) was the infamous Roman Emperor whom his contemporaries believed to be the instigator of the fire that destroyed most of the city. As the blaze raged it is said that he sang to his lyre and recited his own poetry whilst enjoying the spectacle from the top of a high tower. Many historians doubt his complicity, however, and Nero himself blamed the Christians.

Rome was not built in a day

Great achievements, worthwhile tasks and the like are not accomplished without patient perseverance and a considerable passage of time. This was originally a Latin proverb and has been quoted ever since, as in:

> Rome was not bylt on a daie (quoth he) and yet stood Tyll it was fynysht
>> John Heywood (c. 1497–c. 1580), *A dialogue conteinyng the number in effect of all the prouerbes in the englishe tongue* (1546)

Rome was the greatest city in the ancient world and, according to legend, was founded in 753 BC by the legendary Romulus (hence the city's name) and his twin brother Remus. However, it is most likely to have been named from the Greek *rhoma* meaning strength, and its other Latin name is Valentia, from *valens* meaning strong. As an indication of its importance in the world, Rome features in numerous old sayings such as 'When in Rome do as the Romans do' and 'All roads lead to Rome' – or 'All roads lead to rum', as WC Fields (1880–1946) put it.

Rose by any other name, a

The name of a person is irrelevant; it is their qualities, their personality, that are important. A mere name has no effect upon the characteristics of the person or thing in question. Or 'A chrysanthemum by any other name would be easier to spell', as William J Johnston once commented. The phrase is from Shakespeare:

> JULIET: What's in a name? that which we call a rose
>> By any other name would smell as sweet;
>> So Romeo would, were he not Romeo call'd.
>>> *Romeo and Juliet* (1594)

Rose-tinted spectacles, to see through
To look at life or to regard circumstances with unjustified optimism, always looking on the bright side of life, as though it were suffused with a gentle pink light. Spectacles of such a hue would show the world in the pink, but it would be misleadingly rosy, bright and hopeful. The French equivalent is *voir la vie en rose* – to see life 'in the pink', which in turn means to be in excellent health, abbreviated from the phrase 'in the pink of health' or 'in the pink of condition', a meaning derived from a flower in its best state.

Round robin
A petition or protest signed in a circular form on the page so that no one name heads the list. The device is believed to have originated in France and the term could be a corruption of *rond* and *ruban* – round ribbon. The round-robin letter or petition is believed to have been first devised by British sailors in the seventeenth or early eighteenth centuries when presenting a grievance to the ship's captain. To avoid punishment the ringleader would arrange for the signatures to be inscribed in a circular fashion around the page – although if the ship's captain was particularly vindictive he would punish all the signatories for insurrection. A round-robin tournament is a friendly sporting contest, such as tennis, in which all participants change partners so that everyone competes against everyone. A round-robin letter, usually sent at Christmas, is a duplicated letter recording one's news and achievements of the year for the edification of one's acquaintances.

Round-table conference
A conference in which all participants are ranked equally, or at which it is agreed that the discussion or dispute should be settled amicably with the maximum amount of 'give and take' on all sides. King Arthur's Round Table, which seated 150 knights, was circular to prevent any rivalry among the delegates, and the earliest written reference to it is in Wace's (c. 1115–c. 1183) *Roman de Brut* of

1155. The expression came to general prominence in connection with a private conference in the house of Sir William Harcourt in January 1887, with the aim of trying to reunite the Liberal Party after the split caused by Gladstone's support of Irish Home Rule. Other politically notable round-table conferences were those on the future of Indian government held in London in 1931–2.

Round up the usual suspects

Since the film *The Usual Suspects* was released in 1985, this phrase has returned to regular use, and is employed as a jocular instruction to gather a group of people together. It is thought that the line was first spoken in the film *Casablanca* (1943), directed by Hal B Wallis and starring Humphrey Bogart and Ingrid Bergman (although Ronald Reagan and Ann Sheridan were originally named for the leads). Claud Rains, playing the French Captain Renault, Chief of Police in wartime Casablanca, delivers this classic line in the last scene of the movie: 'Major Strasser has been shot. Round up the usual suspects.' When shooting began the script was not finished and towards the end of filming the dialogue was written on demand and literally rushed to the set. According to the film chronicler Leslie Halliwell (1929–1991), the film 'just fell together impeccably into one of the outstanding entertainment experiences in cinema history'. (See also **Bogart – Don't Bogart that joint**, q.v.)

Royal 'we', the

The somewhat superior choice of the collective pronoun 'we' in place of the individual 'I' by a single person. It has long been observed that the Queen has used this style in referring to herself, for instance during her Christmas Day broadcasts, while the frosty comment, 'We are not amused' was attributed to Queen Victoria in 1900. In March 1989, the then Prime Minister, Margaret Thatcher, announced to the world in a famously regal tone:

We have become a grandmother.

Rubicon – To cross the Rubicon

To take an irrevocable step, to burn one's bridges behind one, to go beyond the point of no return. The Rubicon was a small river, possibly the present-day Fiumicino, which formed the border between ancient Italy and Cisalpine Gaul, the province allocated to Julius Caesar. When Caesar, having disobeyed the Senate's order to disband his army and resign his command, crossed this stream in 49 BC he went beyond the limits of his own province and thus became an invader in Italy. With this action he hastened the outbreak of war between Pompey and the Senate, in which Caesar triumphed.

Rule of thumb

A rough guesswork measure, a calculation based on generally held experience in a certain field. This rule is distinct from any proven theory and refers to the use of the thumb to make rough measurements. The first joint of the average adult thumb measures 1 inch or 25mm, and thumbnail sketches are miniature drawings, roughs or diagrams, usually quickly executed. There is also an apochryphal derivation for 'rule of thumb': in the days when it was accepted practice for a man to beat his wife, the stick for this purpose was legally allowed to be no broader than the thickness of a man's thumb; it was illegal for the stick to be thicker and a man using such a stick could be arrested for assault.

Run the gauntlet, to

To be attacked on all sides or to be severely criticized. The expression appeared in English at the time of the Thirty Years War (1618–48) as 'gantlope', meaning the passage between two files of soldiers. It is an amalgamation of the Swedish words *galop* – passageway, *gata* – way, and *lop* – course. 'Running the gauntlet' was a form of punishment used by the Germans, but was said to have originated in Sweden amongst soldiers and sailors. The company or crew, armed with whips, thongs or rods, were assembled in two facing rows, and the miscreant had to run the course between them while each man dealt him as severe a blow as he thought befitted the misdemeanour. The American Indians also had a similar, more brutal, form of retribution, because here the victim was not intended to survive the blows he suffered during his run.

Salt – To rub salt into the wound

To increase someone's pain or shame. The phrase alludes to an ancient nautical punishment for misbehaviour by members of a ship's crew. Errant sailors were flogged on the bare back, and afterwards salt was rubbed into the wounds. Salt is a well-known antiseptic so it helped to heal the lacerations, but it also made them much more painful. An extension of this phrase is the saying 'Don't rub it in', an admission that one may have made a fool of oneself, but people should not carry on reminding one.

Salt – To sit above the salt

To sit in a place of distinction at the dinner table. Formerly the family 'saler' or salt cellar was an ornate silver centre-piece, placed in the middle of the table. Special or honoured guests of distinction sat above the saler, that is, between the salt and the head of the table where the host sat, while dependants and not quite so important personages sat below. Salt is also a significant euphemism, from the early nineteenth century onwards, for one's financial worth, as a play on the word 'salary', or the amount one earned. In Roman times a soldier received part of his pay in the form of a *salarium*, or salary, which was actually an allowance for the purchase of salt (the Latin for salt is *sal*). Salt was not easily obtainable then, and a soldier was not 'worth his salt' if he did not come up to standard, that is, did not deserve his *salarium*. To be 'true to one's salt' is to be loyal to your employers, those who pay your salary.

Salt – With a pinch of salt

To treat information or explanations with great reservation, qualification, scepticism, doubt or disbelief. To make allowance for a mere grain of truth, but not much. To add a pinch of salt to something makes it taste more palatable and helps one to swallow it.

Sands – The sands are running out

A metaphor to remind us that time is short; there will be less time to do what you have to do unless you act now. The phrase is often used with reference to one who has not much longer to live. The allusion is to the sand in an hourglass. The original version of the phrase is 'The sands of time are running out', the first part of which appears in the poem 'A Psalm of Life' (1838) by Henry Wadsworth Longfellow (1807–82):

> Lives of great men all around us
> We can make our lives sublime,
> And, departing, leave behind us
> Footprints on the sands of time.

Or as Robert Burns (1759–96) wrote in 'Tam o' Shanter' in 1791:

> Nae man can tether time or tide.

Sauce for the goose is sauce for the gander, what is

This old phrase seems to promote sexual equality long before it was fashionable. It suggests that the same rules apply in both cases, what is fitting for the husband should also be fitting for the wife. Originally 'sauce', from the Latin *salsus*, means salted food used as a relish with meat, such as pickled roots and herbs. 'Sauce' also means cheek or impertinence, perhaps in relation to the piquancy of such relishes.

Saved by the bell

This is a boxing term thought to date from the 1930s. A floored contestant being counted out (see **Out for the count**, q.v.) might be saved by the ringing of the bell marking the end of the round, giving him the three-minute break between rounds to recover. However, there is another, albeit unsubstantiated, and gruesome theory to explain this phrase. When graveyards became overcrowded in the eighteenth century, coffins were dug up, the bones taken away and the graves reused. In reopening the coffins, one out of twenty-five were found to have scratch marks on the inside, meaning that people must have been buried alive. To guard against this most unfortunate occurrence, a string was tied to the wrist of the corpse, and led from the coffin and up through the ground, where it was tied to a bell. Someone would have to sit in the graveyard all night to listen for the bell – hence the phrase 'saved by the bell'. From the same derivation we have night workers on the 'graveyard shift' and sailors on the 'graveyard watch' between midnight and dawn.

Say it with flowers

This phrase, still used to advertise flowers, was first used by the Society of American Florists in 1917. It is said to have been invented for the chairman of the society's publicity committee, Henry Penn of Boston, Massachusetts. Advertising boss Major Patrick O'Keefe suggested, 'Flowers are words that even a babe can understand', which was a line he had found in a poetry book. Eventually, between them O'Keefe and Penn came up with this winning slogan. The neat phrase has also been the title of several songs.

Scratch, to come up to

To be fully prepared for a challenge, or good enough to pass any test; to make the grade. This is a colloquialism from the boxing ring dating back to the nineteenth century. Under the London Prize Ring Rules introduced in 1839 a round in a prizefight ended when one of the fighters was knocked down. After an interval of thirty seconds the floored fighter was given eight seconds to make his way, unaided, to a mark scratched in the centre of the ring. If he failed to reach the mark, he 'had not come up to scratch' and was declared the loser of the bout.

Sell (someone) down the river, to

This expression means to deceive or to betray. The phrase probably originated in the first few years of the nineteenth century in the southern states of America. Since by then it was illegal to import slaves, there was an internal trade and they were brought down the Mississippi to the slave markets of Natchez or New Orleans. Therefore if a slave was 'sold down the river' he lost his home and family. The saying particularly alludes to the practice of selling unruly slaves to owners of plantations on the lower river, where conditions were harsher than in the northern slave states. To 'sell' is old slang for swindle or hoax, and a person who has been tricked is said to have been 'sold'. To 'sell the pass' is to betray one's own side; the phrase was originally Irish and is applied to those who turn king's evidence or who betray their comrades for money. The tradition relates to the behaviour of the regiment that was sent by Crotha, Lord of Atha, to hold a pass against the invading army of Trathal, King of Cael. The pass was yielded for money and Trathal assumed the title of King of Ireland.

Sell off the family silver

To dispose of valuable assets or heirlooms that have been passed down from one generation to the next, for a much needed injection of cash, having fallen upon hard times. Many such items are traditionally silver, and are of great sentimental value; worse, once gone they cannot be retrieved. The allusion was memorably set into a modern context in a speech by the former Conservative Prime Minister, Sir Harold Macmillan, 1st Earl of Stockton (1894–1986), to the Tory Reform Group on 8 November 1985. In it he criticized Margaret Thatcher's government for privatizing nationalized industries like the railway, gas and electricity companies, when he said, 'First of all the Georgian silver goes, and then all that nice furniture that used to be in the saloon. Then the Canalettos go.' The speech was summarized as 'selling off the family silver'.

Sell-by date, to be past
This term comes from the supermarket and is applied to perishable packaged food on which the date before which, for safety reasons, it should be consumed is indicated. The expression is widely applied metaphorically to almost any short-lived or disposable area of life that may lose its freshness or appeal, such as ideas, fashion, media personalities, relationships; it is sometimes also used of people, especially those in high-profile jobs, such as actors or models.

Send in the clowns
This expression is from the world of showbiz. As it sounds, the phrase comes from the big top, and is a way of saying, 'The show must go on'. In the event of a calamity backstage at a circus the clowns are sent into the ring to keep the audience amused

and distracted until the panic behind the scenes is over. Whatever disasters occur, life must go on as normal and nothing should be allowed to ruin the public reputation of the show. The phrase was used as the title for a song in Stephen Sondheim's musical *A Little Night Music* (1974).

Send (someone) to Coventry, to

To refuse to speak to someone, to ostracize a person or ignore them. At the time of the Great Rebellion (or English Civil War) between 1642 and 1649, it is said that the citizens of Coventry once had so great a dislike of soldiers that a woman seen speaking to one was instantly shunned. Hence when a soldier was 'sent to Coventry' he would get the cold shoulder. During the years of strife between King Charles I and Parliament, Royalists were often attacked and either killed or taken to Coventry, where they would be imprisoned and ostracized, because the city was strongly Protestant and pro-Parliament. Edward Hyde, Earl of Clarendon (1609–74), referred to Royalist prisoners captured in Birmingham who were 'sent to Coventry', effectively into exile. To take this a step further, to refuse to have any dealing with a person or group of people as a means of protest or coercion is to 'boycott' them, which dates from 1880, when such methods were used by the Irish Land League against one Captain CC Boycott (1832–97), a land agent in County Mayo, to try and persuade him to reduce rents.

Serious money

A large amount of money, a substantial fee or a five- or six-figure salary. A frequently heard phrase during the high-earning, high-spending years of the materialistic 1980s, Caryl Churchill wrote a satirical play of this title in 1987. Ambitious, enterprising and successful executives expect to earn 'serious money', and there are many different phrases attached to this sentiment: 'If you pay peanuts you get monkeys' or 'You get what you pay for' or 'We're talking telephone numbers'. (The last metaphor only works provided you are not just dialling the operator – 100 – or other 3-digit numbers.

Seventh heaven, to be in

To be supremely happy, in a state of complete ecstasy. The seventh heaven was defined by the Cabbalists who were students of a Jewish mystical system of theology and metaphysics dating from the eleventh and twelfth centuries, but with roots in ancient Greek teachings. They interpreted passages from the Old Testament based on the symbolism of numbers, devised and decoded charms and created mystical anagrams and the like. They maintained that there are seven heavens each rising above the other, the seventh being the home of God and the archangels, the highest in the hierarchy of the angels. Seven is a mystic or sacred number. It is the sum of four and three which, among the Pythagoreans, were, and have been ever since, counted as lucky numbers. Among ancient cultures there were seven sacred planets, and the Hebrew verb 'to swear' means literally to 'come under the influence of seven things', while in an Arabic curse seven stones are smeared with blood, all of which demonstrate the power of seven as a mystical number.

Sharp end, at the sharp end

Directly involved with the action, positioned where the competition or danger is greatest. The connection is not with the point of a sword, but with the pointed shape of the bows of a ship, which are the first towards the enemy in any engagement or battle. The cry of 'Look sharp!' or 'Sharp's the word!' are both calls to immediate action, whether on the battlefield or in the playground; the expressions also mean to be observant, to 'keep your eye on the ball'. Before the days of large supermarkets and closed-circuit television, if a shopkeeper suspected a customer of shoplifting he would give a coded warning to his assistant by saying, 'Mr Sharp has come in'.

She who must be obeyed

A phrase describing a harridan or domineering woman. It was inspired by its use in John Mortimer's *Rumpole of the Bailey* which was serialized on television in the 1970s and 1980s. The eponymous barrister, Rumpole, famously used this phrase of his overbearing wife. Mortimer's original source was Sir Henry Rider Haggard's (1856–1925) novel *She* (1887), and Denis Healey ironically referred to Margaret Thatcher in this way in 1984. With similar feeling, the phrase "Er indoors' comes from the 1970s television series *Minder*, that being how Arthur Daley (played by George Cole) refers to Mrs Daley.

Sheep – A sheep in sheep's clothing

An amusing modification of the well-known proverb 'a wolf in sheep's clothing', meaning to be spineless or utterly weak. It is attributed to Winston Churchill in a comment on his successor, the Labour Prime Minister, Clement Attlee (1883–1967), although the British writer Edmund Gosse (1849–1928) first used it when referring to the poet T Sturge Moore (1870–1944) in about 1906. In another political taunt Labour's Denis Healey described an attack on him by the Conservative Geoffrey Howe as like being 'savaged by a dead sheep'. The original phrase linking wolves and sheep probably comes from the Bible:

> Beware of false prophets, which come to you in sheep's clothing, but inwardly they are ravening wolves.
>
> Matthew 7:15

Sheep – Separate the sheep from the goats

To divide the worthy from the unworthy, the favoured from the disfavoured, the good from the not so good. The comparison comes from the Bible, and sheep usually symbolize the meek (and stupid, in certain circumstances); in biblical terms, however, they represent the flock of Christ, while goats symbolize virility, lust, cunning and destructiveness.

> And before him shall be gathered all nations; and he shall separate them one from another, as a shepherd divideth his sheep from the goats.
>
> Matthew 25:32

A similar expression, also from the Bible, is 'to separate the wheat from the chaff', meaning to distinguish good from bad, that is the 'staff of life' from the waste material. The comparison is implicit in certain biblical texts:

What is the chaff to the wheat? saith the Lord.

Jeremiah 23:28

Shoes – Another man's shoes

'To stand in another man's shoes' is to take the place of another person. In similar vein the opportunistic phrase 'Waiting for dead men's shoes' is sometimes thought, if not spoken. Among the Vikings when a man adopted a son, the adoptee put on the shoes of his new father.

Reynard the Fox, a medieval beast epic (c.1175–1250), is a satire on contemporary life found in French, Flemish and German literature. Reynard, having turned the tables on the former minister Sir Bruin the Bear, asks the queen to let him have the shoes of the disgraced bear. As a result Bruin's shoes are torn off and put on the new hero.

Short shrift, to give

To treat someone peremptorily and unsympathetically, without heeding any mitigating arguments, or simply to make short work of something. Shrift is defined as a confession to a priest and 'short shrift' refers to the few minutes left to a convict between condemnation, confession and absolution, and then finally execution. To shrive a person is to impose penance after confession so that they can be freed from their sins. Shrovetide is the three days just before Lent when people used to go to confession and afterwards indulged in all sorts of partying. Shrove Tuesday is the day before Ash Wednesday and is known as Pancake Day, when the store cupboards are emptied to mark the beginning of a symbolic period of abstinence, as penance during Lent.

Show a leg, to

The summons to 'show a leg' or 'shake a leg' is a morning wake-up call. It is a naval phrase and was the traditional alarm call used to roust the hands from their hammocks. It comes from the days in the mid-nineteenth century when women were allowed to sleep on board ship when the navy was in port. At the cry of 'Show a leg!' if a woman's limb was shaken out of the hammock she was allowed to lie in, but if the hairy leg of a rating appeared he had to get up and get on with his duties. Later in the nineteenth century to 'shake a leg' came to mean to dance, while in America it meant to hurry up.

Sick as a parrot, as

A banality to describe extreme disappointment at an unexpected failure or setback. It suggests several meanings of the word sick, among them ill, diseased or disgusted, and parrots are extremely prone to viruses such as the highly contagious disease psittacosis (parrot fever). In the 1970s and 1980s it was a somewhat overused metaphor favoured by football managers, who often used it to describe their feelings after losing a match. Despite being mocked by the satirical magazine *Private Eye*, and perhaps helped by the absurdity of the 'Dead Parrot' sketch in *Monty Python's Flying Circus*, its imagery caught the public imagination, and it is now used ironically.

Silk purse out of a sow's ear, to make

To attempt to make something good or of great value from what is naturally bad or inferior in quality. A similar old proverb is that 'You cannot make a horn out of a pig's ear'. To make a pig's ear of something is to bodge it, the ear of a slaughtered pig being its most worthless part, no good for anything. This led to a similar slang expression, thought to have been instigated in the 1920s, 'to make a dog's breakfast', or 'dog's dinner', out of something. If a person is described as looking like a dog's dinner, they are considered to be 'done up to the nines', or vulgarly overdressed.

Sixty-four-thousand-dollar-question, the
The ultimate and most difficult question, the nub of a problem. This widely used phrase comes from the 1940s American radio quiz show, *Take It or Leave It*. During the course of the show contestants were asked increasingly difficult questions for prize money, which also increased as the questions became harder. The final question was worth $64. Inflation has affected this expression over the years since it began life as the humble sixty-four dollar question, growing first to sixty-four thousand and recently to sixty-four billion. The expression is used in all English-speaking countries.

Skeleton in the closet
A domestic source of humiliation or shame which a family or individual conspires to conceal from others. Every family is said to have one, and certainly these days it seems that every public figure has one too, whether it is in the form of an ex-mistress or lover, inhaling marijuana smoke, or not, at university, or some ancient but discreditable financial scam. An apocryphal story has it that a person without a single care or trouble in the world had to be found. After a long search a squeaky-clean lady was found, but to the great surprise of all, after she had proved herself on all counts she went upstairs and opened a closet which contained a human skeleton. 'I try and keep my trouble to myself, but every night my husband makes me kiss that skeleton,' she said. She then explained that the skeleton was that of her husband's rival, killed in a duel over her. The expression seems to have been in use at least since the mid-nineteenth century, when it appeared in *The Newcomes* by William Makepeace Thackeray (1811–63):

And it is from these that we shall arrive at some particulars regarding the Newcome family, which will show us that they have a skeleton or two in their closets as well as their neighbours.

Skid row, to be on
An American expression applied to the part of town frequented by vagrants, hobos, alcoholics, or down-and-outs. Hence if you are 'on the skids', it means that you are on your way to that rather grimy quarter of the city, about to skid off the path of virtue. The expression probably comes from the early days of the Seattle timber industry. A 'skid row' was a row of logs down which other felled timber was slid or skidded. Tacoma, near Seattle, became prosperous with the growth of the timber industry, and in due course there were plentiful supplies of liquor and brothels in the town, close at hand for lumberjacks working the skid row.

Sling your hook!
A somewhat forceful command urging a person to leave, or a way of asking someone to go away without resorting to foul language. The expression is probably of nautical origin and alludes to the anchor, or 'hook', which must be secured in its sling at the bow before the ship can cast off. Shortened forms of the expression 'Hook it!' and 'Take your hook!' are also used, perhaps to give more emphasis to one's wish that a person should leave and set about their business. It is possible, however, the hook may be an angler's hook, since to be 'on one's own hook' means to act on one's own initiative – a hook is cast into the water to make a catch or, metaphorically, to achieve something useful.

Small is beautiful
Originally the title of a book (1973) by EF Shumacher (1911–77), this has become a catchphrase for those opposed to large industrial conglomerates and overbearing bureaucracy in government, and who desire economics on a human scale. It is thought that Shumacher, who was subsequently celebrated as a business guru, did not invent the phrase, but that his publishers came up with it, possibly influenced by the power of the phrase 'black is beautiful'. It can now be used in almost any context along with the phrase 'less is more', which implies both refinement and minimalism.

Smoke-filled room

This is a political euphemism (see also **Beer and sandwiches**, q.v.) and refers to the meeting rooms from which political leaders emerge, ideally with a decision or resolution, after many hours of negotiating or horse trading. However, nowadays the rooms are unlikely to be filled with smoke, as the habit of smoking has become extremely unfashionable with its well-known health risks.

The original smoke-filled room was a suite in the Blackstone Hotel in Chicago, in which Warren Harding was selected as the Republican presidential candidate in June 1920 after protracted bargaining. The phrase itself appears to have come from a comment by Harding's chief spokesman, Harry Dougherty, and in those days the smoke was likely to have been that of cigars.

Snug as a bug in a rug, as

A whimsical and comfortable comparison dating from the eighteenth century, although a snug is a sixteenth-century word for a parlour in an inn. The phrase is usually credited to Benjamin Franklin (1706–90), who was very fond of children and wrote these words to Georgiana Shipley, the daughter of his friend, the Bishop of St Asaph. As a gift from Philadelphia Franklin's wife had sent the Shipleys a grey squirrel whom they called Skugg, a common name for squirrels at the time. Tragically he escaped from his cage and was killed by a dog. Franklin wrote this epitaph in 1772:

Here Skugg
Lies snug
As a bug
In a rug.

However, there are earlier uses, as in a celebration of David Garrick's (1717–79) Shakespeare festival in 1769, seen printed in the *Stratford Jubilee*:

> If she [a rich widow] has the mopus's [money],
> I'll have her, as snug as a bug in a rug.

In 1706, Edward Ward (1667–79) wrote in *The Wooden World Dissected*

> He sits as snug as a bee in a box.

And in Thomas Heywood's (c. 1574–1641) 1603 play *A Woman Killed with Kindness* there is:

> Let us sleep as snug as pigs in pease-straw.

Sour grapes

This is an ancient metaphor for something that seems desirable, but is, in fact, unattainable and for that reason is disparaged or rubbished; in other words, that which you cannot get. The phrase comes from the well-known fable by Aesop (6th century BC), 'The Fox and the Grapes'. One hot day a thirsty fox spotted some juicy-looking grapes hanging from a vine. The cluster of fruit was just out of reach and however hard he tried he could not reach the grapes, and the greater the effort he made the hotter and thirstier he became. Eventually the fox gave up and reasoned that as the grapes were beyond reach they would probably be sour and inedible. The moral of the story is that we can console ourselves with the fact that if some things are unattainable, we probably wouldn't like them anyway. A fine example of the sour-grapes syndrome is by William Penn Patrick:

> Those who condemn wealth are those who have none and see no chance of getting it.

And according to Ovid (43 BC–AD 17):

> Envy assails the noblest: the winds howl around the highest peaks.

Spanish custom, an old Spanish custom

Also known as 'an old Spanish practice', this is the bargaining excuse given by workers trying to bend the rules when it comes to negotiating certain advantages, such as more pay, shorter working hours, more tea breaks, and so on. It is not clear why the Spanish are blamed for this. However, historic national rivalry between the Spanish and the British has led to many light-hearted expressions in the workplace, such as the 'Spanish worm', which is a nail hidden in a piece of wood against which a carpenter jars his chisel or saw. To be given the 'Spanish archer' is to be sacked or given the 'elbow', and Spanish workers, or indeed anyone who procrastinates or takes their time over things, are, whether fairly or unfairly, accused of carrying out their business *mañana* – tomorrow. Perhaps this relates to the custom of the Spanish siesta – which comes from the Spanish words *sexta hora*, sixth hour – when work stops in the heat of the early afternoon and everyone has a nap, during what the British consider to be part of the working day.

Spin doctor

This is an American idiom which was first applied in political commentary in the mid-1980s under Ronald Reagan's presidency, describing his public-relations advisers during promotion of the 'Star Wars' Strategic Defence Initiative (SDI). These so-called 'spin doctors' were on 'spin control', their mission being to give the preferred interpretation of events to the world's media, thereby manipulating public opinion in the desired direction. The phrase comes from baseball and refers to the spin put on the ball by a pitcher to disguise its true direction or confuse the batter. The spin doctor is now a prominent feature in British politics and business in general.

Stand by your man

This is the title of a song by American country and western singer Tammy Wynette (born Virginia Wynette Pugh, 1942–98) and first recorded in 1968:

Stand by your man,
And show the world you love him,

Keep giving all the love you can,
Stand by your man.

Tammy Wynette was dubbed 'The First Lady of Country', but despite entitling her 1979 autobiography *Stand By Your Man*, she had five marriages and suffered chronic illness, arson attacks, kidnapping and bankruptcy. The phrase has entered the language, and is used by headline writers when alluding to such stalwart wives as Hillary Clinton and various Tory spouses who stood by their men despite much-publicized philandering by their husbands.

Star-Spangled Banner, the

The flag of the United States of America, otherwise known as the Stars and Stripes. The stripes represent the original thirteen states, and the fifty stars the states that now make up the Union. The flag is also popularly called 'Old Glory', so named, supposedly, by William Driver, a Salem skipper, in 1831. At the outset of the American Revolution each state adopted its own flag; however, in 1776 a national flag of thirteen red and white stripes, with crosses of St George and St Andrew in a canton, was adopted. By act of Congress in June 1777 the new flag had thirteen alternate red and white stripes with a union of thirteen white stars arranged in a circle on a blue field, representing a new constellation; it was apparently designed by Francis Hopkinson. In 1794, after the admission of Vermont and Kentucky, the stripes and stars were increased to fifteen, but in 1818 it was decided to restore the thirteen stripes, and that stars should be added to signify the number of states in the Union; the stars were also squared up for the first time. 'The Stars and Stripes Forever' is the name of John Philip Sousa's most popular military-band tune, and 'The Star-Spangled Banner' was adopted as the official anthem of the United States in 1931.

The words were written by Francis Scott Key (1780–1843) in 1814 and the tune was that of 'Anacreon in Heaven', a popular drinking song composed by a Londoner, JS Smith (1750–1836).

Stiff upper lip

A determined resolve combined with complete suppression of the emotions. This is supposedly a traditional characteristic of the English, especially military officers during the two world wars, their upper lips frequently concealed with a moustache, which perhaps became fashionable because it could conceal any uncontrollable trembling reflexes at the wrong moment. A quivering upper lip is often a sign of emotion. It is not sure when the phrase was first heard, but it appeared well before the First World War in the petry of Phoebe Cary (1824–71) in 'Keep a Stiff Upper Lip':

> And though hard be the task
> 'Keep a stiff upper lip'.

Still waters run deep

However quiet or calm someone may seem on the surface, do not be deceived, there is probably great depth of knowledge, personality or hot temper lurking below. This is a Latin proverb, and the Malayan proverb, 'Don't think there are no crocodiles because the water is calm', means much the same. It is never a good idea to show off or talk too much, because as everyone knows, empty vessels make the most noise. Speech is silver, but silence is golden. Ducks on a pond illustrate this proverb perfectly, in that they glide smoothly across the surface, without a feather out of place, but below their feet are paddling – nineteen to the dozen. However, it can be argued that still waters do not run at all.

Stir-up Sunday

In the Christian calendar, this is the last Sunday after Trinity Sunday and takes its name from the collect, the short Anglican prayer for the day, 'Stir up we beseech thee, O Lord, the wills of the faithful people.' It was an old custom to let everyone in the family stir the Christmas plum-pudding mixture on this day and make a wish, hence the old children's rhyme as a play on the

prayer, 'Stir up we beseech thee, the pudding in the pot.' For best results Christmas puddings should be made well in advance so that the fruit can soak up the brandy and whisky, and the mix requires much stirring. Before electric food processors, involving the whole family in the effort was an efficient way of spreading the work.

Stone, to cast the first
To be first to criticize, to find fault, to start a quarrel, or to cast aspersions on someone's character. To cast means to throw a missile, and the barbaric custom of capital punishment in biblical times was to pelt heretics, adulteresses and criminals with stones and rocks in a public place. The phrase is from John 8:7, spoken by Jesus to the Scribes and Pharisees who brought before him a woman caught in adultery. They said that according to the law of Moses, she should be stoned to death, to which Jesus replied:

> He that is without sin among you, let him first cast a stone at her.

Strike while the iron's hot

To act immediately when the opportunity arises. This is a metaphor from the blacksmith's shop, since iron cannot be easily worked once it has cooled down. The phrase has been attributed to Geoffrey Chaucer (c. 1345–1400), although there are many ancient sayings that encourage action today rather than waiting for tomorrow (see **Carpe diem**, q.v.) Pittacus said 'Know thy opportunity', and **Make hay while the sun shines** (q.v.) appears in an early sixteenth-century book of proverbs. More up to date, a women's-lib slogan neatly inverts the proverb in a warning against inaction, 'Don't iron while the strike is hot'.

Suck it and see
Said of anything experimental, the saying alludes to taking a pill which has to be sucked first to see if it works. The expression was

a catchphrase of Charlie Naughton of the Crazy Gang (*fl.* 1930s) and probably originated earlier in the music halls. It sounds rather old-fashioned nowadays, with the American meaning of the word 'suck' taking hold in Britain. To say that something 'sucks' is a derisive description of something bad or of someone's failure. A 'sucker' is someone who is easily deceived, a greenhorn; that is, a new-born creature that still suckles at its mother's breast.

Suits you, sir

This is one of many catchphrases that entered the language in the 1990s, and comes from the popular BBC television comedy series *The Fast Show*, starring Paul Whitehouse and Charlie Higson, in which two tailor characters repeat the phrase leeringly, 'Ooh! Suits you, sir. Ooh'. With a further surreal touch, the phrase is now used by the same two characters in a television commercial for a brand of lager. Other daft catchphrases include, 'Does my bum look big in this?' 'I've always admired the music of Frank Sinatra' and 'I'm a little bit weeeeyyyy . . . a little bit tasty . . .'. As comedy writers in the late 1980s, Whitehouse and Higson invented the comic characters Stavros and Loadsamoney for fellow comedian Harry Enfield.

Sunny side up

This is a visual metaphor used to describe how a fried egg should be served. It is a phrase that came from American diners and is urban shorthand when ordering a fried egg. Eggs are served with the yolk 'sunny side up', or can be cooked on the other side and served yolk down, that is, 'easy over'.

Sweet Fanny Adams

This expression is ambiguously used to mean either nothing at all, or sweet nothing. It has a very tragic origin. In 1867 eight-year-old Fanny Adams was raped and murdered in a hop garden in Alton, Hampshire, and her dismembered body was thrown into the River Wey. A twenty-one-year-old solicitor's clerk, Frederick Baker, was tried soon after and hanged at Winchester. The Royal Navy, with extreme black humour, adopted the poor girl's name as a synonym for tinned mutton which was first issued at this time, and for a while stewed meat was known as Fanny Adams. Sweet Fanny Adams became, as a consequence, a phrase for anything worthless, and subsequently to mean nothing at all. The phrase is still used today usually as just the initials 'SFA' or 'sweet FA', which happen to be the same as 'f**k all', from which most people think this expression is derived.

Sword of Damocles, the

Impending danger or disaster in the midst of great prosperity or good fortune. In the fourth century BC, Damocles, who was a toadying sycophant of Dionysus the Elder of Syracuse (see **Walls have ears,** q.v.), was invited by the tyrant to test his self-proclaimed charm and wit. Damocles accepted and was treated to a sumptuous banquet, but over his head a sword was suspended by a mere hair, intended by Dionysus as a symbolic indicator of the fragility of wealth and power, his own included. This quite naturally inhibited Damocles's performance at the banquet because he was too frightened to move.

Talk turkey, to

To discuss some subject frankly or seriously.
The origin of the expression is uncertain, but it may have arisen from the efforts of turkey hunters to attract their prey by making gobbling noises. The stupid birds would then either emerge from their cover or return the call, so revealing their whereabouts. At the turn of the last century, the turkey was considered an amusing bird, and

159

conversations in which one 'talked turkey' were convivial. A young suitor's chat-up lines would also be called 'talking turkey', perhaps because in a fit of nerves he might become tongue-tied and his words would come out like gobbling noises. Later the meaning became more serious and related to stern admonitions. Incidentally, turkeys do not come from Turkey, but from North America and were brought to Spain from Mexico. Benjamin Franklin suggested the turkey should be the emblem of the United States of America – however, the bald eagle was chosen instead.

Tall-poppy syndrome

This expression is believed to come from Australia and means to cut an overtly superior person down to size. The phrase has been current since 1931 when Jack Lang (1876–1975), the left-wing leader of the New South Wales administration, described egalitarian policies as 'cutting the heads off the tall poppies'. It derives from the legend that Tarquin, King of Rome (534–510 BC), symbolically demonstrated his wishes for the captured city of Gabii by decapitating the tallest poppies in his garden; accordingly the leading citizens were executed.

Tango – It takes two to tango

A frequently used axiom that comes from the 1952 song of this title by Hofmann and Manning:

> There are lots of things you can do alone!
> But it takes two to tango.

This satisfyingly alliterative phrase is often used in a sexual context when one partner is accused of seducing the other and it implies willingness on both sides. It is also used more widely in the fields of business and politics, to imply that, in order to achieve agreement between two groups, both may have to compromise.

Tarred with the same brush, all tarred with the same brush
Everyone in the group alike is to blame, all sharing the same failings, all sheep of the same flock. This old saying alludes to the former treatment of skin complaints, sores and the like in sheep, with a brush dipped in tar. In less racially enlightened days, not in fact so long ago, the expression, 'a touch of the tar brush' described a person of mixed race, pointing out the not-quite-white colour of their skin.

Teddy-bear syndrome

This describes the characteristics of someone who gets married or enters a relationship simply because he or she fears being alone and needs the constant presence of a comforter, the function of a teddy bear for many small children. The teddy bear is thought to have been so called after American President Theodore (Teddy) Roosevelt (1858–1919), who enjoyed bear hunting. The toy acquired its name after a presidential bear-hunting expedition in 1903. To ensure the President made a kill, the organizers stunned a small brown bear and tied it to a tree.

Teeth – By the skin of one's teeth

By the narrowest margin. There are several metaphors with the possible meaning 'only just' and many allude to bodily parts, emphasizing the physical danger of a given situation from which one might have just escaped. Teeth have no skin and therefore the action or task that has been achieved has been done so 'by a hair's breadth'. This is a biblical phrase that means to have suffered a 'close shave':

> My bone cleaveth to my skin, and to my flesh, and I am escaped with the skin of my teeth.
>
> Job 19:20

Thick as thieves, as
To be intimate with some person or group, to be in collusion with them. Thieves notoriously conspire and plot together, and devise secret languages so that they can discuss their business in a code that will not be understood by others, a slang or jargon that used to be known as 'thieves Latin'. Cockney rhyming slang itself was originally a closed language to the uninitiated and was created by crafty East Londoners to outwit authority and eavesdroppers. 'Thick' is used in this context to mean closely knit, not in its other meaning of stupid, a bit slow on the uptake. To be 'as thick as two short planks' states the obvious, for when one plank is placed on another the result is twice as thick as a single plank.

Third degree, to be given the
This is to be the object of detailed cross-questioning to get to the bottom of an inquiry, whether it be criminal or general. In America the term is applied to the use by the police of exhaustive questioning in an endeavour to extort a confession or incriminating information from a suspect, criminal, accomplice or witness. 'Third-degree treatment' is also used as a euphemism for torture.

This week's deliberate mistake
A phrase generally used in a facetious way to admit that an error has been made. It dates back to a 1938 BBC radio programme, *Monday Night at Seven*, during which a mistake was inadvertently made. Thousands of listeners pointed the *faux pas* out to the BBC. With some positive thinking, the producer decided to develop the idea and the 'deliberate mistake' became a regular feature of the programme, spawning a new catchphrase, 'Did you spot this week's deliberate mistake?'

Throw in the sponge, to
To throw in, or throw up, the sponge means to give up, to admit defeat. The metaphor is from the boxing world and refers to a second, from the boxer's corner, tossing a sponge, used to refresh his contestant in between rounds, towards the centre of the ring, to signify that his man is beaten. To 'throw in the towel' also means

to concede defeat in boxing, for a second might also literally throw a towel into the ring to show that the game is up.

Thunder, to steal one's
To adopt someone else's own special methods or ideas as if they were one's own. The story behind the origin of this phrase was recounted by the eighteenth-century actor and playwright Colley Cibber (1671–1757), in his *Lives of the Poets*, and was also mentioned by Alexander Pope (1688–1744) in his poem 'The Dunciad'. John Dennis (1657–1734), an actor-manager of the early part of the eighteenth century, had invented a machine to make stage thunder, which he employed in his own play, *Appius and Virginia*, performed at the Drury Lane Theatre in London in 1709. Mr Dennis, whatever his inventive talents, was a not particularly gifted playwright; the play did not fill the house and was soon taken off in favour of a production of *Macbeth* by another company. Dennis went to the opening night and was astonished to hear his thunder machine in action. He leapt to his feet and shouted, 'That is my thunder, by God, the villains will play my thunder but not my play!' Since the eighteenth century the phrase has subsequently been refined to become 'to steal one's thunder'.

Tickety-boo, all tickety-boo
There are many phrases for this enthusiastic statement that everything is 'fine and dandy', or 'all shipshape and Bristol fashion'. 'Tickety-boo' may come from the word 'ticket' as in 'that's the ticket'. In the nineteenth century charities issued tickets to the poor that could be exchanged for soup, clothing and coal. Also at that time, the busy port of Bristol enjoyed a high reputation for efficiency in preparing ships for sea.

To acknowledge the corn
An American expression meaning to confess or own up to a charge, or to admit failure to deliver. In a Congressional debate in

1828 one of the states claiming to export corn admitted that the corn was actually used to feed hogs, and exported not as corn, but inside the animals' digestive systems.

Today is the first day of the rest of your life
Despite the fact that this well-used phrase has a New Age ring, it originated in 1969 at the Syanon anti-drug and alcohol centres. It is believed to have been coined by Charles Dederich, the founder of the centres, and it swiftly became a mantra with a somewhat evangelical flavour, reflecting the 'take-it-day-by-day' approach to curing addictions to anything from cigarettes or food to sex or drugs.

Too many cooks spoil the broth
A well-known proverb meaning that too many opinions on a matter become self-defeating. The adage has been in use since the sixteenth century, if not before. For almost every proverb or nugget of wisdom, however, there is usually another that means precisely the opposite, the usual riposte for 'Too many cooks spoil the broth' being 'Many hands make light work'. Groucho Marx (1895–1977) commented, 'I'm going to stop asking my cooks to prepare broth for me. Over the years, I've found that too many broths spoil the cook.'

Torch, to carry a
To suffer unrequited love. The torch represents the flame of undying love, and the implication is that the emotion is long standing and either not returned or undeclared. A torch singer is (usually) a female who sings sentimental love songs in this vein.

It is thought that 'torch song', in this sense, may have been coined by Tommy Lyman in the 1930s. The film *Torch Singer* (1933) was about an unwed mother who sings in a night club, while *Torch Song* (1953) told the story of a musical-comedy star's love for a blind pianist; later the play *Torch Song Trilogy* (1982) by Harvey Fierstein tackled the more taboo subject of homosexual love.

Turn on, tune in, drop out

This is the mission statement of the hippie movement from about 1967. Turn on to drug use, tune in to new values – reject those of your parents, and drop out – of society. It was used as the title of a 1967 lecture by Dr Timothy Leary (1920–96) and he explored the theme further in his book *The Politics of Ecstasy*. Towards the end of his life Leary attributed the phrase to the Canadian media guru Marshall McLuhan (1911–80). An amusing variation on the theme, known as 'the LSD motto', was:

Turn on, tune in, drop dead.

Turn the tables, to

To reverse a situation and put one's opponent in the predicament that one has been suffering. The saying was recorded in the early seventeenth century and was applied to a popular card game in which a player, if he found himself at a disadvantage, might reverse the position of the board and thus shift the disadvantage to his opponent. The phrase may also come from the old custom of reversing the table or board in games of chess or draughts so that the opponents' relative positions are altogether changed. Another apocryphal theory relates to arguments in Roman marriages. Roman gentlemen were given to buying expensive tables, and if the man had previously chided his wife for making a costly purchase she would 'turn the tables' and remind her spouse of his own extravagance. On a different tack, 'table-turning' is the mysterious phenomenon of the turning of tables without the evidence of any mechanical force, which in the early days of spiritualism was commonly practised at séances. It was said by some to be the work of departed spirits, and by others to be the result of influences such as mesmerism.

Turn-up for the books, a
A piece of luck or unexpected good fortune. This phrase comes from the world of betting on the horses. The 'book' is the record of bets laid on a race and is naturally kept by a 'book'maker, commonly known as a bookie. When the horses do not run to form and the favourite does not win, it's a good day for the bookie and he can line his pockets; for him it's 'a turn-up[wards] for the books'.

Under the counter
This phrase originated during the Second World War, and describes a then very common practice among tradesmen with an eye to the main chance. From the outbreak of the war many items, ranging from the basics like eggs, butter, meat and jam to 'luxuries' such as petrol, silk stockings and chocolate, were rationed. Dishonest tradesmen would keep articles and foodstuffs that were in short supply out of sight or 'under the counter', for sale to favoured customers, usually at inflated prices. This form of trading was part of the thriving wartime black market, and the term is still used today to describe any illicit trading.

United we stand, divided we fall
A political slogan of the state of Kentucky that dates back to the late eighteenth century. The line appeared in a 1768 song called

'The Patriot's Appeal' by Jonathan Dickinson:

> Then join hand in hand, brave Americans all!
> By uniting we stand, by dividing we fall.

The idea can be traced back to 550 BC and Aesop's fable of 'The Four Oxen and the Lion'. And in St Mark's Gospel (3:5) we find:

> If a house be divided against itself, that house cannot stand.

Vorsprung durch Technik

This translates from the German as 'advancement through technology', and was used as an advertising slogan for Audi cars in Britain from 1982. The use of a German phrase which few could understand was apparently designed to emphasize to British buyers that the Audi was a German car and hence a reliable, quality product. In Britain it succeeded as an intriguing slogan, perhaps thanks to the deadpan delivery on the commercial by the actor Geoffrey Palmer, although it only had a minor success as a commonly used catchphrase. The line was used as a morale-boosting dictum to Audi's workers and was written up over the gates of the factory in Germany.

Walk the plank, to

To be put to the supreme test or, worse, to be about to die. 'Walking the plank' is a nautical term for a punishment involving being made to walk blindfold along a plank suspended over the ship's side and eventually landing up in the drink as shark food. It was a pirate custom of disposing of prisoners at sea in the seventeenth century. The practice is probably more familiar in fiction than in fact, however, since pirates would have been unlikely to kill off captives, who could have been sold as slaves or ransomed. In RL Stevenson's (1850–94) novel *The Master of Ballantrae* (1889) James Durie and Colonel Francis Burke enlist with the pirates who capture their ship, but the brigands make their other prisoners walk the plank. And Captain Hook, in JM Barrie's (1860–1937) *Peter Pan and Wendy* (1912), threatened to flog Wendy and the Lost Boys with a cat 'o' nine tails and then make them walk the plank.

Walls have ears, the

This is a warning to watch what you say, or what secrets you divulge, wherever you are, because someone might be listening. In the time of Catherine de Medici (1519–89), certain rooms in the Louvre Palace, Paris, were said to be constructed to conceal a network of listening tubes called *auriculaires*, so that what was said in one room could be clearly heard in another. This was how the suspicious queen discovered state secrets and plots. The legend of Dionysus's ear may also have been the inspiration for this audiovisual play on words. Dionysus was a tyrant of Syracuse (see **Sword of Damocles**, q.v.) in 431–367 BC, and his so-called 'ear' was a large ear-shaped underground cave cut in a rock that was connected to another chamber in such a way that he could overhear the conversation of his prisoners.

Wash one's hands of, to

To abandon something, to have nothing to do with some matter or person. The allusion is to Pontius Pilate's washing his hands at the trial of Jesus. Pilate was the Roman governor of Judaea (from AD 26–36) who tried Jesus. Although he found Christ not guilty, he washed his hands of the matter, bowing to the pressure of Jewish religious leaders, and sentenced Jesus to be crucified.

> He took water and washed his hands before the crowd, saying 'I am innocent of this man's blood, see it yourselves.'
>
> Matthew 27:24

We shall overcome

An American protest slogan since the beginning of the twentieth century. It originated as a part of a song in pre-Civil War times and was adapted in about 1900 by C Albert Tindley as a Baptist hymn, 'I'll overcome some day', which became famous in 1946 when black tobacco workers sang it on a picket line in Charleston, South Carolina. Pete Seeger (1919–) and other protest singers added verses, and in the early 1960s it became the main US Civil Rights anthem:

Oh deep in my heart, I know that I do believe,
We shall overcome some day.

Wham bang, thank you ma'am

This rather vulgar expression was originally used by American forces during the Second World War. The phrase was later employed mostly by women to describe short and meaningless sexual intercourse, or perhaps a one-night stand. It is now used contemptuously for any selfish act of male gratification at women's expense.

What a carve-up

This is an English slang phrase meaning to spoil someone's chances, or to have all prospects ruined. A 'carve-up' also means in criminal circles to share out illicit booty. On the road it means to cut aggressively in front of another driver, one of the actions that has led to the phenomenon of 'road rage'. There are now all sorts of 'rage' situations to describe the frustrations of modern life, such as 'trolley rage' in the supermarket, or 'air rage' demonstrated by drunken passengers on an aeroplane.

What the Dickens?

An exclamation of disbelief, akin to 'What the devil?' There is still some hesitancy in using such a strong oath and the phrase is often shortened to 'What the . . .?' 'Dickens' here is probably a euphemism, possibly in use since the sixteenth century, for the devil, otherwise known as Satan or the Prince of Evil, and has nothing do to with Charles Dickens (1812–70). In Low German its equivalent is 'De duks!' which may have become altered in English to 'dickens'.

> I cannot tell what the dickens his name is.
> Shakespeare,
> *The Merry Wives of Windsor* (1600)

'To play the dickens' is an old-fashioned expression meaning to be naughty, or act like a devil.

What you see is what you get (WYSIWYG)

This is a phrase from the world of computers, usually shortened to the acronym WYSIWYG, and suggests that what ones sees on the computer screen is exactly how the material will look when printed. It has probably been in use since the mid-1960s, although only widely used from the 1980s . Now the expression is used even more broadly by public figures who want to persuade an audience that they are not trying to hide anything or deceive by appearances. President Bush quoted the phrase on the first day of the Gulf War, 16 January 1991, when asked how he was feeling.

Where there's muck there's brass

An encouraging phrase to make one roll up one's sleeves and get to work; otherwise a statement that where there is dirt there is money. Feeding the soil, harvesting the crops, mining the coal may make your hands dirty, but they can produce untold riches. The saying has come to be associated with the grimy mining and manufacturing industries of the north of England, following the Industrial Revolution of the late nineteenth century, many of which brought their owners substantial wealth. Francis Bacon (1561–1626) probably had a more charitable meaning in mind when he wrote, 'Money is like muck, not good except to be spread.' A more modern colloquial phrase is, 'It's a dirty job, but someone's got to do it', but this phrase has more of a 'grin-and-bear it' attitude.

Where's the beef?

Advertising slogan meets political catchphrase. The American Wendy hamburger chain's 1984 television commercial showed a group of elderly women looking at the small hamburger of a competitor on a huge bun – they all admired  the bun, but the unimpressed third woman asked, 'Where's the beef?' Later in 1984, when Walter Mondale was seeking the Democratic presidential nomination, he famously quoted the slogan to describe what he thought was lack of substance in the policies of his rival, Gary Hart. In America the phrase is also used to mean 'Where's the problem?'

White man's burden, the

In the imperialistic days during the wide influence of the British Empire, from the mid-nineteenth century, white races, especially the British, believed it to be their duty to govern, educate and generally enlighten the so called 'backward' coloured peoples of the world. It is now inconceivable that such a condescending and racist attitude should have taken so great a hold. The phrase comes from a poem by Rudyard Kipling (1865–1936) of the same title (1899):

> Take up the White Man's burden –
> Send forth the best ye breed –
> Go bind your sons to exile
> To serve your captives' need.

To ask someone to 'play the white man', that is to be a 'good sport' or 'good egg' about some minor dispute or misunderstanding, or in some personal crisis, is an ironic reference to the imperial days when a person of honourable character or good breeding was described as a 'real white man'.

Who breaks a butterfly on a wheel?

To put great effort into accomplishing a small or unimportant matter. The phrase comes from Alexander Pope's (1688–1744) poem 'An Epistle to Dr Arbuthnot' (1735):

> Satire or sense, alas! can Sporus feel?
> Who breaks a butterfly upon the wheel?

The allusion is to an ancient form of torture, 'breaking on the wheel', in which the long bones of a convict are broken with an iron bar, counterpointed with the delicacy of a butterfly. Famously,

in 1967 the editor of *The Times*, William Rees-Mogg, caught the public mood when he defended Mick Jagger after his three-month prison sentence for possession of illegal drugs, in an editorial headlined with this quotation. Technically Rees-Mogg was in contempt of court for commenting on the case before it had gone to appeal, but the fact that he was not even publicly admonished testifies to the general support for his stand.

Who dares wins

The motto of the SAS (Special Air Service Regiment) appears to have been borrowed from the Alvingham barony, created in 1929. The SAS was founded by Captain (later Colonel Sir) David Stirling in 1941, and its origins therefore lie in the Second World

War. The motto became famous after members of the crack regiment successfully stormed the Iranian embassy in London in May 1980, ending its occupation by terrorists and freeing their hostages. A feature film about the exploits of the SAS was produced, with the motto as its title, in 1982, and the *Daily Mirror* labelled its bingo promotion 'Who Dares Wins' in the same year.

Willow, to wear the

For those unlucky in love, to grieve for a lost lover, or pine for an absent sweetheart. The willow, especially the weeping willow, has long been associated with sorrow, and is taken as an emblem of desolation or desertion. Thomas Fuller (1608–61) wrote, 'The willow is a sad tree, whereof such as have lost their love make their mourning garlands,s and the psalmist tells us that the Jews in captivity hung their harps upon the willows in sign of mourning':

> By the waters of Babylon, there we sat down and wept when we remembered Zion.
> On the willows there we hung up our lyres.
>
> Psalms 137:1, 2

Wind – It's an ill wind that blows nobody any good

This is an old adage to encourage 'positive thinking'. It means that it has to be a very great misfortune from which someone does not benefit, or in other words that someone will always profit by every loss. It all depends on your outlook in life, the cup is either half empty or half full. The allusion is nautical, and arises because a headwind for one ship will be a tailwind for another sailing in the opposite direction.

Wind – To sail close to the wind

This is another of the many proverbs that come from life on the high seas. It is a figurative expression, still in use today, and means to take a chance, to emerge from an escapade just within the letter of the rule book, or, more riskily, to push the limits of what decency or propriety allows. This nautical expression refers to the practice of steering a ship as near as possible to the point from which the wind is blowing while keeping the sails filled. To 'sail against the wind' is to go against the trend, in opposition to current thinking, practice or fashion. And to 'sail before the wind' is to prosper, to meet with great success, just as a ship sails smoothly and rapidly with a following wind. Similarly, to 'sail into the wind' is to attack or reprimand someone forcefully, or to tackle a task with great vigour and directness.

Wing – On a wing and a prayer

To chance it, to hope for the best and have faith, with perhaps only small chance of success. It is a matter of interpretation as to whether the wing referred to here is that of an aeroplane or a more celestial being. The phrase comes from a Second World War song by Harold Adamson (1943), based on the actual words spoken by the pilot of a damaged aircraft who radioed the control tower as he prepared to come in to land. The song runs:

> Tho' there's one motor gone, we can still carry on
> Comin' in on a wing and pray'r.

Even in his moment of panic the pilot might have been inspired by words from Psalm 104 (v.3):

> Who layeth the beams of his chambers in the waters:
> and maketh the clouds his chariot, and walketh upon the wings
>   of the wind.

Word – My word is my bond
The motto of the London Stock Exchange since 1801. At the
Stock Exchange bargains are made on the 'nod' without a written
pledge being given, and without documents being exchanged. The
motto's Latin form is *Dictum meum pactum*, and the phrase implies
a sense of honour, an agreement that cannot be broken without
disgrace.

Writing on the wall, the
This is not graffiti, but a bad sign, a portent, often foreshadowing
trouble or disaster. The metaphor is biblical in origin and comes
from Daniel 5:5–31, where King Belshazzar, while he was feasting,
found out about the forthcoming destruction of the Babylonian
Empire through the mysterious appearance of handwriting on a
wall. The words read in Aramaic, *mene, mene, tekel, upharsin*,
literally, 'numbered, weighed, divisions'. Daniel interpreted these
words as, 'You have been weighed in the balance and found
wanting,' thereby predicting the king's downfall and that of his
empire. Indeed, Belshazzar was killed that night, and his kingdom
was conquered.

Wrong side of the tracks, to be on the
To be born on the wrong side of
the tracks is definitely a
disadvantage, for the area was that
part of town which was deemed
both socially and environmentally
inferior. The expression originated
in America and refers to the fact
that, formerly, poor and industrial
areas were often located to one

side of the railroad tracks, not least because the prevailing wind
would blow smoke and smog in that direction, leaving the better-
off neighbourhoods unpolluted; in addition, industry needed to be
close to the railroad, and so workers' housing was also established
near those areas. The poorer districts of British cities are often east
of the city centre for this reason, since the prevailing wind is
usually west or south-west.

Years – The first seven years are the hardest

A cliché usually offered as wise advice about a marriage or a new job, implying that the first stages will be the worst and that things can only get better. It probably comes from First World War parlance, 'Cheer up, the first seven years are the worst,' referring to the length of regular service in the army. Seven years is a traditional period for change, and seven is a holy or mystic number: there are seven days in a week, seven ages of man and seven dwarves (see **Seventh heaven**, q.v.). *The Seven-Year Itch* was a play written by George Axelrod in 1952, which became a film starring Marilyn Monroe (1926–62) in 1955. The title has been in use as a catchphrase ever since and is applied especially to husbands, who have a tendency to wander from the marriage after seven years. The word 'itch' has been used since the seventeenth century as a slang word for a sexual urge.

You ain't seen nothin' yet

This was Ronald Reagan's presidential catchphrase in 1984, which he used repeatedly in his successful bid for re-election. Always happy to quote from movies, he featured the line in his victory speech. It is also the title of a 1974 song by Bachman-Turner

Overdrive, the Canadian pop group, which is the ironic theme tune to 'Smashy and Nicey', the comic radio DJs played by Paul Whitehouse and Harry Enfield in the latter's TV comedy show. The original phrase 'You ain't heard nothin' yet' is most famously attributed to Al Jolson (1886–1950) in the first full-length 'talkie' movie, *The Jazz Singer*, in 1927. It was the title of one of Jolson's songs, written by Gus Khan and Buddy de Sylva in 1919, but he had also used the song title as a catchphrase in his stage act before the film was made.

You are what you eat
An informal slogan with 'alternative-lifestyle' overtones that dates back to the 1960s, and the title of a film shown in Britain in 1969. The idea behind the phrase is not new. In *Psychologie du Goût* (1825) Anthelme Brillat-Savarin (1755–1826) wrote, 'Tell me what you eat and I will tell you what you are.' In 1945 the diarist Sir Henry 'Chips' Channon (1897–1958) fondly commented on the death of Sir Harcourt Johnstone, Liberal MP, bon viveur and Minister for Overseas Trade:

> He dug his grave with his teeth.

You're never alone with a Strand
A classic sixties television commercial with a moody style that is still admired today, although when it was shown it failed to achieve its aim of actually selling Strand cigarettes. In 1960, John May of the SH Benson agency conceived the idea for an advertisement to appeal to the youth market by using a moody Frank Sinatra/James Dean lookalike who strolled through a lonely location in a raincoat and hat. The actor soon had his own fan club and the theme tune became a hit. However, viewers did not rush out and buy the cigarettes, perhaps associating them with the loneliness and rejection of youth. Tobacco advertising on television is now banned in Britain.

You've come a long way, baby
In 1968 it was still perfectly acceptable to smoke cigarettes, and this slogan for the campaign by Virginia Slims was targeted at

women, cashing in on the feminist mood of the times. The phrase was then used on Women's Lib posters. To call a girl 'baby' is a term of affection, especially in America; however, in the late 1990s the politically incorrect phenomenon known as 'laddism' resulted in young girls being called 'baby' or 'babe' in a leering, ironic fashion. Fast sports cars are known as 'babe magnets', especially attractive girls are referred to as 'hyper-babes' or '*über*-babes' and Lara Croft, voluptuous virtual heroine of the *Tomb Raider* computer games, is known as a 'cyber-babe'. The phrase is also the title of the 1999 best-selling album by Fat Boy Slim.

You've never had it so good

A strident phrase used by the Prime Minister, Harold Macmillan (later first Earl of Stockton; 1894–1986), in a speech at Bedford in July 1957. He specifically phrased his speech not to sound boastful, but to act as a warning that the prosperity of the post-war years would be difficult to maintain; however, it was taken out of context and used to label him as complacent, interested only in material comforts.

> Let's be frank about it. Most of our people have never had it so good. . . . What is beginning to worry some of us is, 'Is it too good to last?' . . . Can prices be steadied while at the same time we maintain full employment in an expanding economy? Can we control inflation?

Macmillan is said to have adopted the phrase after it had cropped up in conversation with Lord Robens, a former Labour minister, shortly before his speech. However, 'You never had it so good' was already a political soundbite that had been used by the Democrats in the American presidential election of 1952.

Your country needs you

The most famous recruitment slogan ever – inseparably linked with
the poster showing Field-Marshal Lord Kitchener (1850–1916)
staring out with pointing finger. Kitchener was appointed Secretary
of State for War on 6 August 1914, two days after the outbreak of
the First World War, and it was his job to build up the numbers of
recruits for the 'New Armies'. Eric Field of the small Caxton
advertising agency wrote the original line for the posters, 'Your
King and Country need you', appealing to all patriots. The idea
was widely imitated abroad, and in America, which joined the war
on the Allied side in 1917, Uncle Sam pointed his finger out of a
poster bearing the legend 'I want you for the US Army'.